Colonial America

VOLUME 2

CABOT—DETROIT

CONSULTANT EDITOR: DR. D. THORP

Published 1998 by
Grolier Educational, Sherman Turnpike, Danbury, Connecticut 06816

© 1998 Brown Partworks Ltd

Set ISBN: 0-7172-9193-6
Volume ISBN: 0-7172-9195-2

Library of Congress Cataloging-in-Publication Data
Colonial America.
p.cm.—Includes bibliographical references and index.
Contents: v. 1. A-By—v. 2.C-De—v. 3. Di-Ga—v. 4. Ge-In—
v. 5. In-Marq—v. 6. Marr-Na—v. 7. Ne-Pe—v. 8. Ph-Re—
v. 9. Rh-St—v. 10. St-Z.

1. United States—History—Colonial period, ca. 1600–1775—
Encyclopedias. Juvenile. 2. United States—History—Revolution,
1775–1783—Encyclopedias. Juvenile. I. Grolier Educational (Firm)
II. Title: Colonial America
E188.C696   1998
973.2—DC21   97-44595
                                                      CIP
                                                       AC

For information address the publisher:
Grolier Educational, Sherman Turnpike, Danbury, Connecticut 06816

FOR BROWN PARTWORKS LTD
Editor: Clint Twist
Designer: Bradley Davis
Picture research: Sharon Southren
Text editor: Mike Sharpe

Printed in Singapore

CONTENTS

Cabot, John 84

California 85

Cartier, Jacques 88

Champlain, Samuel de 90

Charleston 92

Cherokee 95

Children 100

Church-State Relations 106

Clothing 110

Colbert, Jean-Baptiste 114

Columbus, Christopher 115

Committees of Correspondence 117

Connecticut 118

Constitutional Convention 122

Continental Army 124

Continental Congress 128

Cornwallis, Lord 130

Coronado, Francisco de 131

Coureurs de Bois 132

Crafts 134

Crime and Punishment 140

De Soto, Hernando 144

Declaration of Independence 145

Deerfield Massacre 148

Delaware 149

Detroit 151

Further Reading 152

Set Index 152

C JOHN CABOT

▲ *John Cabot and his son Sebastian embarking on his ship the* Matthew *in May 1497 for his historic voyage across the Atlantic.*

John Cabot was born in Genoa, Italy, around 1450 and was given the name Giovanni Caboto. In 1461 his family moved to Venice, where he embarked on a career as a sailor. Caboto, like many 15th-century adventurers and spice merchants, was eager to find an overseas route from Europe to the Orient. Inspired by Columbus's voyage of 1492, Caboto believed the quickest route to the Orient lay to the west across the Atlantic. After failing to secure financial support in Spain for his expedition, Caboto moved to London to seek sponsorship there and changed his name to its English form.

IN THE WAKE OF COLUMBUS

In 1496 King Henry VII authorized Cabot to search for new lands, and he secured financial backing from local merchants. On May 2, 1497, the *Matthew* and a crew of 18 set sail from Bristol, reaching either Labrador or Cape Breton Island on June 24. Believing he had found the coast of China, Cabot claimed the territory for the English king. On his return to Bristol he reported that the new land was temperate and its sea full of fish. Anxious to break their dependence on Icelandic fishermen, English merchants funded a second voyage, and in May 1498 Cabot sailed with five ships and 200 men.

One of the ships was forced to turn back to the west of Ireland, but the fate of the remaining ships, including Cabot himself, is still uncertain. Some believe they sailed west to Greenland then south to Labrador and as far as Chesapeake Bay, and that Cabot returned home empty-handed and died in obscurity. Others think that Cabot and his crew were all lost at sea.

Although he did not find a western route to the Orient, Cabot discovered the rich fishing banks of northeast North America and helped establish the idea that a continent to the west divided Europe from the Orient.

SEE ALSO
COLUMBUS, CHRISTOPHER

CALIFORNIA

Years before the first English colonists set eyes on North America, Spanish adventurers were roaming up and down the Pacific coast. In 1542 an expedition led by Joao Rodriques Cabrillo sailed up the coast from Baja (Lower) California to modern-day Monterey Bay. Cabrillo died in January 1543, but his expedition pressed northward as far as what is now named Oregon.

The Spanish gave the name California to this entire region. "California" was in fact the name of an imaginary island that first appeared in a popular story written in 1510. The author located it "on the right hand of

The barren mountains of the Sierra Nevada and the desert beyond provided a natural barrier to European exploration. Settlement during the colonial period was confined to more fertile plains along the coast.

A native fisherman from southern California, as depicted in a book published in London in 1726 called A Voyage around the World.

the Indies" and filled it with gold and a race of mythical women who lived without men. There was certainly gold in the region, but the Spanish were as unsuccessful in finding that as they were in finding the mythical women.

The real inhabitants of the area were Native Americans, and there were many tribes, including the Hupa and the Yurok. California was home to between 250,000 and 300,000 natives during the 18th century, a greater population density than anywhere in North America. The favorable climate of much of California meant a relatively abundant and varied supply of food, and the tribes lived by hunting, gathering, and fishing in the rivers and off the coast.

FORGOTTEN LAND

In 1579, during his epic voyage around the world, the English sailor Sir Francis Drake landed at the point known as Drake's Bay, just north of San Francisco, to carry out repairs to his ship the *Golden Hind*. In his five weeks there Drake and his men had peaceful encounters with the local Coast Miwok natives and left behind a brass plate claiming Nova Albion (New England) for Queen Elizabeth.

The English made no attempt to exploit their claim, and for nearly two centuries the Spanish, too, stayed out of the area, content to confine themselves to Mexican territories. Spanish Jesuits did begin establishing a string of missions in Baja California as early as 1697, but the authorities in Mexico City made no effort to settle Alta (Upper) California until the 1760s.

What caused this belated interest were the Russian explorers in Alaska who, the Spanish thought, presented a threat to their territory. In order to defend the northern frontiers of New Spain, the Spanish built a series of forts, known as presidios. Between 1769 and 1782 presidios were built at San Diego, San Francisco, Monterey, and Santa Barbara. Although they were intended to provide protection from foreign invaders as well as native attacks, these forts remained small. In 1794 the total number of soldiers in all four presidios was only 218.

While it was the Spanish military who encouraged the settlement of Alta California, the years of Spanish occupation in the New World had taught them the value of "civilizing" the native populations. To the Spanish this meant converting natives to the Christian religion, so wherever the Spanish military established a presence, Franciscan missionaries tried to spread Christianity. In all, 20 Franciscan missions were founded in Alta California before Spanish rule in the region was brought to a close by Mexican independence in 1821.

ON A MISSION FROM GOD

The Franciscans made strenuous efforts to convert the native people to Christianity, and by 1820 more than 20,000 of them were residing in missions. They were instructed in Christian beliefs, and more importantly to the Spanish they also provided a free labor force to work in the fields.

While the Franciscans viewed the mission system as an attempt to improve the spiritual and moral condition of the natives, it had disastrous effects. The natives became

◄ *Throughout the 16th century most encounters between Europeans and Californian natives were friendly. This contemporary engraving shows an explorer being honored with a tribal headress in about 1570.*

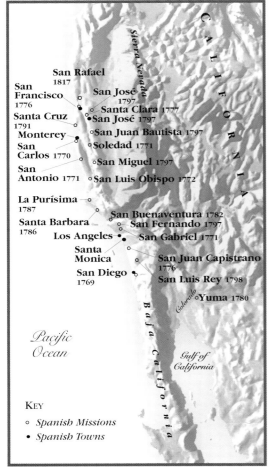

San Rafael 1817

San Francisco 1776

San José 1797

Santa Clara 1777

San José 1797

Santa Cruz 1791

Monterey

San Juan Bautista 1797

San Carlos 1770

Soledad 1771

San Antonio 1771

San Miguel 1797

San Luis Obispo 1772

La Purísima 1787

San Buenaventura 1782

Santa Barbara 1786

San Fernando 1797

Los Angeles

San Gabriel 1771

Santa Monica

San Juan Capistrano 1776

San Diego 1769

San Luis Rey 1798

Colorado Yuma 1780

Sierra Nevada

CALIFORNIA

Pacific Ocean

Baja California

Gulf of California

KEY
- ○ *Spanish Missions*
- ● *Spanish Towns*

▲ *The Mission San Diego de Alcala, built in 1769, was the first of the Spanish missionary settlements founded during the colonial period.*

◄ *Between 1769 and 1821, 20 Franciscan missions had been established in Alta California.*

completely dependent on the mission and isolated from their communities. Apart from some religious instruction, no attempt was made to educate them. They were forced to live in cramped, unhealthy hovels, and many fell victim to European diseases to which they had no immunity—life expectancy for a mission recruit was no more than 10 years. The Spanish population was almost entirely male, and native women were frequently physically abused by soldiers and civilians. The Franciscans deplored this but did little to stop it.

Spanish rule in the region was brought to a close by Mexican independence in 1821. As this era came to an end, ambitious, adventurous Americans began to dream of a nation stretching from the Atlantic to the Pacific

SEE ALSO
DRAKE, SIR FRANCIS ■ MISSIONARIES
■ NEW SPAIN

C JACQUES CARTIER

Cartier was born in 1491 in St. Malo, a port on the coast of Brittany, France. During the 1530s he explored and mapped much of the northeastern region of America.

Since the beginning of the 16th century French fishermen had been visiting the rich fishing grounds off the coast of modern Newfoundland; indeed, Cape Breton Island was later named by the Brittany fishermen who cured their catch on its shores. The first organized exploration of the area was prompted by the French king Francis I, who, like English and Portuguese monarchs before him, was seeking the prestige and riches that would be the reward of finding a fast route to Asia.

BY ROYAL DECREE

In 1534 Francis commissioned Cartier to find a northwest passage to the Indies. With two ships and 61 men Cartier sailed up the Gulf of St. Lawrence, named the surrounding land "New France," and claimed it for his king. He was befriended by Native Americans, probably Iroquoians, who captured his imagination with stories of the Kingdom of Saguenay, which they claimed was rich in precious jewels and spices. With the winter drawing in on the St. Lawrence, Cartier decided to delay his exploration of the region and returned to St. Malo with two natives, arriving there on September 5, 1534.

On May 19 the following year Cartier set sail with three ships, and on September 1 he reached the

▼ Cartier was one of the most skilled navigators and seamen of his generation.

mouth of the St. Lawrence River. Continuing west, he reached the Island of Orleans, which the natives called the Kingdom of Canada— *canada* was the native word for village. Leaving his ships, Cartier traveled on in smaller longboats and on October 20 arrived at the village of Hochelaga, situated on the site of the modern city of Montreal. The Lachine rapids prevented him from continuing further upriver, and he passed the winter at the mouth of the St.

Charles River. Though 25 of his men died, Cartier was determined to find the legendary Kingdom of Saguenay. The following spring he returned to France, arriving on July 16, 1536, with 12 natives who could repeat their tales to the king.

King Francis believed that Cartier's Kingdom of Saguenay would provide him with a colony that contained riches to rival the Spanish colonies in Mexico, and in 1541 he sent Cartier on his third and final trip to New France, this time with five ships. The voyage was under the joint command of the Sieur de Roberval, who was charged with establishing a settlement in New France. Though Roberval did

▲ *When Cartier first encountered natives in the Gulf of St. Lawrence, he treated them with suspicion. However, once a mutual trust had been established the relationship between French and natives prospered for over 200 years.*

◀ *Cartier lands at Perce Rock, Gaspé, in 1534 and claims New France in the name of his king.*

not arrive until the following year, Cartier set up camp at Cap Rouge near present-day Quebec City and explored the Saguenay River. The exotic kingdom proved to be simply wilderness; Cartier returned to France with what he thought were gold and diamonds but turned out to be worthless iron pyrites and quartz crystals. Since there appeared to be no route to the Indies through Canada, the French king refused to fund further explorations.

In 1543 Roberval was recalled to France, and Cartier retired to St. Malo. He died in 1557. Though his colony failed, Cartier's explorations of the St. Lawrence River and his dealings with the natives laid the groundwork for the fisheries and fur trade that would follow. He also established a friendly relationship with Native Americans, in contrast to the hostility that some of the later generations of colonial Americans often showed in their dealings with the native peoples.

SEE ALSO

CABOT, JOHN ■ IROQUOIS ■ MONTREAL ■ NEW FRANCE ■ QUEBEC CITY

SAMUEL DE CHAMPLAIN

Samuel de Champlain was born around 1567 in the French town of Brouage on the Bay of Biscay. He was descended from a long line of seafarers and continued in the family tradition by embarking on a career in the French navy. Champlain fought in Henry IV's religious wars, and in 1599 he joined a Spanish expedition to the West Indies where he was one of the first to suggest constructing a canal through Panama to the Pacific Ocean.

In 1603 he was appointed geographer to an expedition under Aymar de Chatte, Lieutenant General of New France. During this voyage Champlain charted the course of the St. Lawrence River as far as present-day Montreal. When de Chatte died in 1603, his patent (an official royal warrant) was transferred to Pierre Sieur de Monts. Champlain returned to the New World with him in 1604 with the intention of establishing French colonies. While exploring and charting the North American coast

▼ *This map of the Gulf of St. Lawrence was drawn by Champlain, who mapped much of the northeast of North America.*

from the Bay of Fundy in Nova Scotia to Cape Cod, Champlain created the most accurate maps that had been produced up to that date. His first attempt to establish a settlement had little success, and after enduring a brutal winter at the mouth of the St. Croix River, Champlain relocated to Port Royal on the Bay of Fundy, now known as Annapolis. The settlement was attacked by the Virginian Samuel Argall in 1613, forcing many of the French settlers to flee, but those who remained eventually managed to rebuild the town.

Meanwhile, under Champlain's advice the French were turning their attention from the agriculture and fishing of the Bay of Fundy to the potential fur trade on the St. Lawrence River. Champlain recognized the river's key position as an artery into the fur-rich lands of the interior. He formed an alliance with the local Huron Native Americans, helping them fight against the rival Iroquois tribes to ensure that the Huron were masters of the river and thus provided the major link between the fur-trapping tribes of the interior and the French colonial traders.

A GROWING EMPIRE

In 1607 Champlain returned to France with the aim of convincing Sieur de Monts to found a new colony on the river. King Henry IV was eager to establish the name of his country in the New World, and although he provided no direct financial support, he did grant Champlain a monopoly over the fur trade in the

Champlain's first meeting with the native Canadian tribes, with whom he formed an alliance.

C

Champlain was wounded in a skirmish with the Iroquois in 1615 and gave up exploration. In 1629 Quebec was captured by an English raiding party, and Champlain was imprisoned and sent out of the colony; some believe he went to England, others to France. In 1632 the colony was restored to France under the treaty of St. Germain-en-Laye; Champlain returned to govern it until his death on Christmas Day 1635.

A TRUE PIONEER

A soldier, sailor, scholar, explorer, map-maker, and artist, Champlain was among the most gifted of North America's founders. He helped to establish the city of Quebec, and the friendships he forged with the Huron laid the foundations for the alliances between French and native forces against the British and the Iroquois.

SEE ALSO

ACADIA ■ FUR TRADE ■ HURON ■ IROQUOIS ■ NEW FRANCE ■ NOVA SCOTIA ■ QUEBEC CITY

colony. With the two vessels Champlain mustered for the Atlantic crossing, he embarked on his fourth voyage to the New World and on July 3, 1608, established the crucial colony and trading post of Quebec. Three years later, in 1611, Champlain founded a second colony, further west at Montreal, as an outpost against the Iroquois. For the next few years he explored the inland waterways of southern Ontario and northern New York state, traveling as far west as Georgian Bay in Lake Huron. He also named Lake Champlain during this time.

Champlain's heavily fortified residence in Quebec, where he lived between 1616 and 1633. Note the cannon in the courtyard and the firing portholes set into the walls.

ABITATION.DE QVEBECQ

CHARLESTON

Charleston, situated on the coast of South Carolina, is one of the most historically significant cities of colonial America. The first English settlement in South Carolina was established in 1670 at Albemarle Point on the left bank of the Ashley River. It was governed by William Sayle, who had previously been the governor of the Bermuda Islands in the Atlantic. Named "Charles Town" (after King Charles II), the settlement moved in 1680 to a nearby peninsula between the Ashley and Cooper Rivers, a location that was both easy to defend and accessible to large ships. This site became the base from which Charles Town grew. The settlement received its charter (an official document recognizing its status as a city) in 1783 and has since been called Charleston.

During the early years of the Charleston settlement the population thrived by trading with the native tribes, but also survived occasional hostile encounters with them. By 1704 the city had been heavily fortified, and its inhabitants successfully fought off an attack by Spanish and French forces in 1706. The threat of attack had largely disappeared by 1740, and for most of the following century the city enjoyed great prosperity.

GOLDEN YEARS

The wealth of the settlement was based on the large volumes of rice, indigo, and deerskins that were exported through the Charleston docks, but the importation of slaves from Africa also played an important role. Charleston became the largest and wealthiest city in the south, with a vigorous social and cultural life. It boasted its own newspaper, a subscription library, the first American museum, and, on Dock Street, one of the earliest American theaters. Local merchants and planters who had made their fortunes in trade built grand townhouses, a number of which

▼ *The colonial settlement at Charleston occupied a commanding position on the Ashley River.*

still survive in the heart of modern Charleston. Among the most unusual are the late 18th-century merchants' houses of "Rainbow Row" on East Bay Street, so-called because they are painted in a range of striking colors. There are other 18th-century private houses on Church Street, and also the famous Heyward-Washington House built in 1771 by the rice planter Daniel Heyward. Daniel's son Thomas was one of those who signed the Declaration of Independence, and in 1791 George Washington spent a night as a guest at the house.

THE PRIDE OF THE SOUTH

Other colonial monuments in Charleston include the Old Powder Magazine, built in 1713, St. Michael's Cathedral (1761), the Old Exchange and Provost Dungeon (1771), and the Meeting Street building that now houses the Gibbes Museum of Art. Along the Ashley River there are the remains of colonial plantations, but Drayton Hall (1738–1742), a brick building in the Georgian style, is the only mansion to survive in its original form. Nearby are the famous gardens of the Magnolia Plantation, first planted in the late 17th century.

During the years before the outbreak of the Revolutionary War Charleston was the most important southern center of opposition to

British rule. In the final months of 1775 a "Patriot Council of Safety" had taken control of the city, and the last royal governor, Lord William Campbell, had fled. The first state constitution was ratified by the provincial congress at Charleston in 1776. Fortifications were hastily erected, and in June 1776 a British attack was driven off. In 1779 another British assault led by General Augustine Prevost failed to take the city, but in 1780, as part of a full-scale invasion of the south, the British besieged Charleston by land and sea. On May 12, 1780, the city was forced to surrender, remaining under occupation until the British withdrawal in December 1782.

Citizens of Charleston played an important part in the events of this

▲ *Rainbow Row, a series of colorful houses built between 1740 and 1789 for wealthy merchants in the East Bay district of Charleston.*

▼ *The riverside moorings and warehouses of Charleston at the middle of the 18th century. The busy town and port had a population of 8,000 by 1760.*

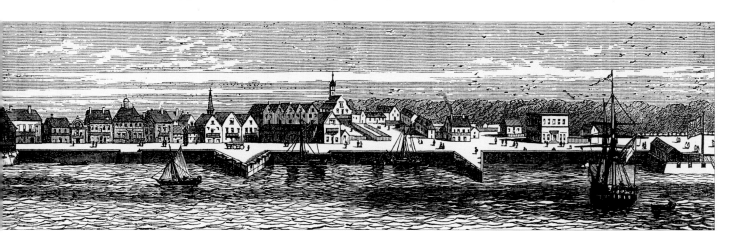

period. The merchant Henry Laurens led opposition to the enforcement of the Stamp Act of 1765, and later became president of South Carolina's first provincial congress, of the council of safety, and of the second Continental Congress.

Following the British assault on Charleston in 1776 the fort on Sullivan's Island was renamed after William Moultrie. Moultrie also defended Charleston in 1780, and became a prisoner of war after its capture. He served as governor of South Carolina in 1785–1787 and 1794–1796.

The most celebrated Charleston citizen of the period is John Rutledge. An outstanding politician and lawyer, Rutledge was a member of the Stamp Act Congress and the Continental Congresses. During the Revolutionary War, as president of South Carolina's General Assembly, he proved to be a strong-minded political leader. After the war he returned to his work as a lawyer; at the high point of his career, in 1795, George Washington nominated him for the position of Chief Justice of the Supreme Court, but the Senate committee rejected the appointment because of his opposition to Jay's Treaty.

SEE ALSO
CONTINENTAL CONGRESS ■ DECLARATION OF INDEPENDENCE ■ JAY, JOHN ■ NORTH CAROLINA ■ SOUTH CAROLINA ■ STAMP ACT CRISIS ■ WASHINGTON, GEORGE ■ YORKTOWN, BATTLE OF

ASSAULT ON CHARLESTON

Early in June 1776 Admiral Sir Peter Parker's fleet arrived off the coast of Charleston with the aim of capturing this important southern port for the British. On board the ships an invasion force led by Sir Henry Clinton prepared to battle with the defense force of 6,000 soldiers under the command of General Charles Lee. Strategically, the key point was the fort on Sullivan's Island, which commanded the entrance to Charleston harbor. On June 9, after disembarking on nearby Long Island, the British army tried but failed to assault Sullivan's Island. Consequently, on June 28, Parker's fleet attempted a direct assault, but the sturdy fortifications withstood a barrage of enemy shells. By contrast, the fort's cannon, despite a shortage of gunpowder, inflicted serious damage on the British vessels. After a 12-hour engagement Parker's ships withdrew, and on June 29 they returned to New York. The heroes of the day were the fort's commander, Colonel William Moultrie, and Sergeant William Jasper, who retrieved the shot-away flag and replanted it on the ramparts.

CHEROKEE

The Cherokee tribe was one of the largest and most important of North America; since the 18th century it has been the largest tribe in the southeast. A member of the Iroquoian family, the Cherokee lived in the Great Lakes area until local Iroquois and Delaware tribes drove them southeast to the Allegheny and Appalachian region of present-day Tennessee, Georgia, Alabama, and the Carolinas. The Cherokee way of life had much in common with their neighboring tribes in America's southeast—the Seminole and Creek, for instance. During the 18th century, however, frequent contact with colonists meant that their culture became more and more Europeanized. The Cherokee traditionally grew crops such as corn, beans, and squash, and they hunted bear, deer, and elk to provide meat for food and skins for clothing. Tools such as knives, axes, and chisels were made of stone before the Europeans introduced them to metal. They were also highly skilled in the crafts of basketry and pottery.

MEDICINE MEN

Nineteenth-century writings have taught us much about traditional Cherokee medicine. They believed that many illnesses were caused by the spirits of animals in revenge for the way humans treated them. Illness and disease were treated according to the cause, not the symptoms shown by the patient; native doctors used herbal remedies, special chants, and magic formulas to try and cure a sick member of the tribe. The Cherokee performed many other rituals relating to their spiritual beliefs, for which they wore ancient ceremonial costumes

such as feathered cloaks and head-dresses. A traditional eagle dance is still performed every year by modern-day Cherokee.

The Cherokee lived in shelters constructed from bark and cane covering a framework of poles or in simple log cabins that they copied from those of the settlers. The seven clans of the Cherokee tribe were divided into small communities

▲ *A Cherokee Chief known as "Stalking Turkey," with a scalping knife in his hand. This picture was painted during his visit to London as a guest of King George in 1762.*

C

containing up to 60 dwellings. These communities were either red (war) clans or white (peace) clans. The red communities dealt with matters to do with warfare, while the white communities attempted to maintain alliances and offer protection to people fleeing from feuds—it was forbidden to shed blood in a white clan. By the mid-17th century there were about 200 Cherokee villages, with a total population of about 22,000. By the early 18th century that population had been halved by smallpox, a disease that arrived in America with European settlers and to which the Cherokee had no resistance.

Throughout the 18th century, as European nations battled for control of the New World, the Cherokees moved between the French frontier at Louisiana, the Spanish frontier at Florida, and the British frontier along the eastern Atlantic coast. They traded with unauthorized French fur traders, and the Cherokee were among several tribes that visited settlements in

▶ *A modern reconstruction of a 16th-century Cherokee building. There are a number of everyday cooking utensils on the table in the foreground.*

▼ *The distribution of Native-American tribes in the southeast in about 1700, before European settlers and the U.S. government drove them west.*

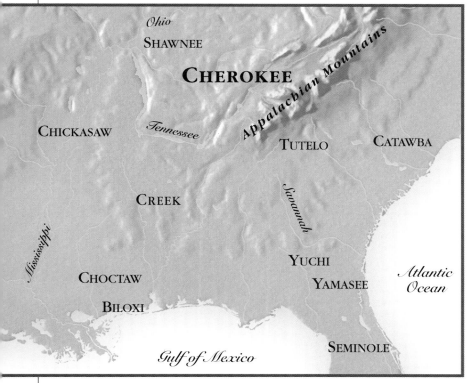

Virginia and the Carolinas, such as Charleston, to barter for goods. They offered furs, skins, and prisoners taken in tribal wars, whom the colonists could sell or use as slaves.

A ROYAL ALLEGIANCE

Britain soon recognized the importance of the Cherokee in its struggle for dominance in North America and tried to make them its allies. In 1721 the Cherokee made an agreement with the governor of the Carolinas, Sir Francis Nicholson, giving him some land and creating a boundary between their two lands. In 1730 Sir Alexander Cuming, a representative of King George II, persuaded the Cherokee to swear allegiance to the British king. He also took some of the tribal chiefs to

England, where they agreed to deal only with British traders and to help them in any confrontation with France.

In 1740, seven years after James Oglethorpe founded the colony of Georgia, he convinced a group of Cherokees under Chief Kalanu to join a campaign he was leading against the Spanish at St. Augustine, Florida. Though the campaign was unsuccessful, the Cherokee involvement showed their willingness to unite with the British. The British tried to encourage Cherokee loyalty by inviting a group of tribesmen to London in 1761. Led by the warrior Outacity, they were personally received by King George III and were courted by London society for several months.

PLOTS AND INTRIGUES

George Washington, then a colonel in the colonial army, realized the importance of cultivating the friendship of the Cherokee, since war between the French and British

▶ *An engraving commemorating the visit of Outacity, the chief of the Cherokee, to England.*

▶ *Members of the 1730 Cherokee delegation to London, wearing European clothes. According to the artist, "They were remarkably strict in their morality, and their behaviour easy and courteous."*

seemed unavoidable. In the French and Indian War (1754–1763) the Cherokee generally supported the British against the French, although there were some disputes within the tribes. At George Washington's suggestion Virginia's Governor Dinwiddie convinced the Cherokee to wage war against the Shawnee of Ohio, who were allied to the French. The Cherokee insisted in return that the British build forts to protect Cherokee families. To fulfill this promise Governor James Glen of South Carolina built Fort Prince George and Fort Loudoun.

The Cherokee expedition against the Shawnee failed, and the alliance between the British and the Cherokee was temporarily broken when 24 Cherokee warriors were murdered by Virginian settlers as they returned to their villages. Inspired by French agents, the vengeful Cherokee turned against the British, raiding settlers on the Virginia and Carolina frontiers and massacring Fort Loudoun. The British retaliated by marching into Cherokee territory, burning the land, and murdering the people. Hostilities between the British and Cherokee continued until 1761, when a peace treaty was signed.

DIVIDED LOYALTIES

At the outbreak of the Revolutionary War in 1775 the Cherokee, believing that the colonists were bent on destroying the forests and colonizing the land, tended once again to side with the British, despite their many disagreements with them. Their support was encouraged by the British with promises of loot from plundered settlements. General Gage in Boston ordered ammunition to be sent to the southern Cherokee tribes so they could continue their raids against the frontier settlements in Virginia, the Carolinas, and Georgia.

TRADITIONAL BALL GAME

THE CHEROKEE, AS WELL AS OTHER TRIBES OF THE SOUTHEAST SUCH AS THE SEMINOLE, CREEK, AND CHOCTAW, PLAYED A TEAM GAME SIMILAR TO LACROSSE.

Usually played between two villages, this native ball game involved two teams of at least 10 men each. The game began with the teams advancing toward each other across the field. A small leather ball was thrown into play by the medicine man.

Each player had two sticks with a net at one end, and the aim was to catch the small leather ball between the sticks and pass it among the team members to get to the goal—a pole at either end of the field. The field was about 150 yds. (140 m) long. A goal was scored by hitting the pole, and the first team to do this 12 times was declared the winner.

▲ Cherokee warriors lying in ambush for British soldiers. During the Revolutionary War the Cherokee tribes were divided, some allied with the colonists while others supported the British.

With the 1783 Treaty of Paris Spain regained Florida, which had been given to the British 20 years earlier after the 1763 Treaty of Paris ended the French and Indian War. The following year, in an effort to unite the southern tribes against the American republic, Spain forged treaties with the tribes in its territory, offering protection if they agreed to deal only with Spanish traders. The Cherokee were mistrustful of the new United States and requested that the Spanish admit them under the treaty.

On November 28, 1785, the Cherokee tribes that remained outside Spanish territory were invited to meet in Hopewell, South Carolina, to negotiate a treaty. The United States promised to prevent any further expansion into Cherokee lands; in exchange the Cherokee were to give up land already settled by Americans. Strict boundaries were drawn, and the Cherokee were invited to send their own deputy to Congress.

Over the next 50 years about 3,000 Cherokees were forced to migrate west beyond the Mississippi. Today there are over 300,000 people of Cherokee descent in America.

SEE ALSO
COUREURS DE BOIS ■ FRENCH AND INDIAN WAR ■ IROQUOIS ■ TREATY OF PARIS, 1763 ■ TREATY OF PARIS, 1783

C CHILDREN

The early settlers rarely mentioned children in their writings, and the information that we do have has been gathered from sources such as parish registers and from the accounts of men such as the Puritan scholar John Robertson. The attitude that existed in many of the devoutly religious settlements is revealed in this passage written by Robertson in 1628: "Children...are a blessing but dangerous...how great and many are their spiritual dangers, both for nourishing and increasing the corruption which they bring into the world with them..."

NAUGHTY FROM BIRTH

The belief that children were basically sinful and naughty from the moment they were born was popular throughout most of Europe during the 17th century. It was the job of parents to teach their children a sense of obedience, self-control, and responsibility. A strict upbringing would keep them from temptation and protect them in the harsh world into which they had been born. In return, children had to obey their parents and treat them with the greatest respect. In Massachusetts in 1648 a law was passed which stated that children over the age of 16 would be put to death if they insulted or struck one of their parents. Although there is no record of this punishment ever being carried out, it shows how seriously the matter was taken.

Quaker communities were generally more open-minded in their attitude to education and child-rearing. They did not believe in violence and so never beat their children. Instead, adults tried to encourage children by setting

a good example to them through their own behavior. They also believed that children were born good and that bad behavior was caused by a child's environment and upbringing.

Children in slave communities were raised according to traditions in African culture, which placed much of the responsibility with the womenfolk. At a very early age children born to mothers on plantations would be cared for by older relatives, since the child's parents worked during the day.

Although there were many different opinions in colonial America about the best way to raise children, settler families were, on the whole, large by today's standards. The birth rate

▲ *A number of children survived the Pilgrim Fathers' difficult journey across the Atlantic in 1620. When they arrived, there was one more child—a baby had been born during the voyage.*

EYEWITNESS

AN 18TH-CENTURY SWEDISH TRAVELER, PETER KALM, BELIEVED THE COLONISTS HAD AN EASY LIFE AND THAT THIS WAS WHY THEY HAD LARGE FAMILIES.

"It does not seem difficult to find out the reasons why the people multiply more here than in Europe. As soon as a person is old enough, he may marry in these provinces without any fear of poverty; for there is such a tract of good ground yet uncultivated that a new married man can, without difficulty, get a spot of ground where he may sufficiently subsist with his wife and children. The taxes are very low and he need not be under any concern on their account. The liberties he enjoys are so great, that he considers himself as a prince in his possessions. I shall here demonstrate by some plain examples...

In the year 1739, on 28 January, died at South Kingston, in New England, Mrs Mary Hazard, a widow in the hundredth year of her age. She was born in Rhode Island and could count altogether five hundred children, grandchildren, great grandchildren and great-great grandchildren."

◀ *An 18th-century portrait of a young boy. There were no clothes specially designed for children, and once they grew out of their long gowns, they were simply dressed as miniature adults.*

during the 17th and 18th centuries was high, regardless of religion or social status. The main reason for this was the plentiful agricultural land in the colonies—there was enough for a man to set up his own farm without having to wait for his father to die to inherit his land. This meant that men and women could marry and start having children at an earlier age than in Europe. Because most of the early colonists depended on farming for their livelihood, the fact that children could help work the land was another good reason for people to raise a large family. Also, it was easy to support a large family when there was so much land.

TEENAGE SOLDIERS

Life in the colonial settlements was often dangerous. Children were regularly called on to defend themselves and their families against native attackers. Young boys were encouraged to become skilled in the use of firearms. The Reverend Joseph Dodderidge, writing in the late 18th century, observed that "A well-grown boy, at the age of twelve or thirteen years, was furnished with a small rifle and a shot pouch. He then became a fort soldier, and had his port-hole assigned him. Hunting squirrels, turkeys, and raccoons, soon made him an expert in the use of his gun."

▶ *Children were expected to attend religious meetings with the rest of the family. They had to sit through sermons that often lasted for three or four hours.*

European traditions also led to large families—parents had always had lots of children so they would be cared for in their old age and there would be children to whom they could pass on their possessions, land, or business.

There were very few effective methods of birth control, and although diseases such as smallpox did not kill as many children as in Europe, settlers continued to raise large families in the belief that many of their children would die at a young age.

THE EARLY YEARS

For the first six years of their lives children were taught to read and write by their parents, who also gave them religious and moral guidance. Most parents were very strict, and beatings were often used as a punishment. Members of the Puritan church believed in "breaking the will" of a child. A minister wrote, "There is in all children… natural pride, which must in the first place be broken and beaten down."

Children were raised by parents in a way that would prepare them for adult life. They were expected to work hard and had little time for play, which was not seen as an important part of a child's life. Very few children had toys, although games such as hopscotch and leapfrog were popular. In the early colonial period most parents were too busy establishing farms, defending their settlements, and improving their simple homes to spend much time with their children,

◀ *The nursery room in the house of a rich Massachusetts family at the end of the 18th century. By this time children were being given more freedom to play during their early years.*

C

▼ Toys were rare, but some did make their way from Europe, like these toy soldiers from France.

and children were often left on their own, looked after by older brothers and sisters.

At the age of only six children were expected to begin working around the home: boys would be given small jobs on the farm, and girls were employed in the kitchen and on other domestic jobs. At this age boys were also given trousers to replace the long "frock" that young children wore. In most families clothes were handed down from older brothers and sisters.

THE IMPORTANCE OF LEARNING
Much emphasis was placed on education, particularly in Puritan communities; in New England in 1642 a law was passed that forced parents to teach their children to read and write, and in the later part of the 17th century schools were built in the established settlements.

There were no enjoyable "teenage years" in colonial society—children were expected to look after themselves from a very early age. At the age of nine or 10 many boys began an apprenticeship with a local

▶ *A romantic view of life on the frontier. From the age of six children were expected to help their parents by working on the land or around the home.*

◀ *Children often slept in the same room as their parents. This reconstruction of a colonial bedroom shows a baby's crib as well as a trundle bed— a small bed that fits underneath the adults' when not being used.*

EYEWITNESS

IN A BOOK HE WROTE IN 1632 AFTER MEETING WITH NATIVE-AMERICAN COMMUNITIES, THE FRANCISCAN MONK FATHER GABRIEL SAGARD DESCRIBED HIS VIEWS ON NATIVE METHODS OF REARING CHILDREN, WHICH ARE VERY LENIENT COMPARED TO EUROPEAN CUSTOMS.

> *Nevertheless they love their children dearly, inspite of...the fact that they are very naughty children, paying them little respect, and hardly more obedience; for unhappily in these lands the young have no respect for the old, nor are children obedient to their parents, and moreover there is no punishment for any fault. For this reason everybody lives in complete freedom and does what he thinks fit; and parents, for failure to punish their children, are often compelled to suffer wrong doings at their hands, sometimes being beaten or flouted to their face. This is conduct too shocking and smacks of nothing less than the brute beast. Bad example, and bad bringing up, without punishment or correction, are the causes of all this lack of decency.*

craftsman such as a blacksmith, carpenter, or barrel-maker, to learn his trade. A boy would usually lodge with the master craftsman for the nine years that an apprenticeship lasted and would learn the skills of the trade through practical experience.

Girls were sent to work as maids and cooks in the houses of richer colonial families, a practice that had been brought from European society. The female children of these wealthy families were more fortunate: until they got married, they were expected to stay at home learning how to manage a household.

By the mid-1700s the influence of the church on childcare, at least among the wealthier classes, was decreasing. Attitudes toward children became more open-minded: parents spent more time with their children and were more willing to show affection. This was partly due to the fact that the standard of living was rising. In the mid-1600s life in colonial America had been literally a fight for survival, but as the European settlements became more established, parents could afford the luxury of devoting more time to the upbringing of their children.

SEE ALSO

APPRENTICESHIPS ■ RELIGION, PURITAN; QUAKER ■ SCHOOLS AND COLLEGES

CHURCH-STATE RELATIONS

Popular American tales often portray colonial America as a land of religious freedom. The story of the Pilgrims tells of a group of persecuted Europeans searching for a land that would allow them greater religious freedom and finally finding it in America. Despite this popular image of America, the basic rights of freedom of religion and the idea of the separation of church and state barely existed before the adoption of the Federal Constitution in 1787. Government interference and religious persecution characterized much of America's early colonial history.

Despite emigrating to America to enjoy freedom of worship, many groups were quick to impose strict controls on religious activity. For example, many churches were directly sponsored by the state, and taxes were imposed to finance the official clergy. Some colonies even prohibited nonchurch members from voting.

KEEPING CONTROL

The Puritan colonies of New England provided a glaring example of this kind of governmental control. Most Puritans settled in America to escape the English Parliament's interference with their religious practices, but they saw no problem with government control in general. One way they did this was by establishing government-

▲ *The Pilgrims created a society based on a strict conformity to the church.*

▶ *In Puritan colonies there were strong links between the church and local government. Anyone opposed to this system or to the Puritans' ideas was strictly punished.*

sponsored churches, which gave the Puritan leaders great influence over the population. The connection between church and state in Puritan New England actually became as strong as it was in England.

NO MERCY

In Massachusetts leaders such as John Winthrop and John Cotton devised a plan to guarantee Puritan control over the government of the colony. This plan stated that only male church members could vote and hold political office. If citizens of Massachusetts disagreed with Puritan ideals, they often suffered at the hands of the colony's government. Religious groups such as the Quakers and the Baptists endured persecution because their ideas differed from Puritan beliefs. In fact, Massachusetts hanged four Quakers in 1660 because they refused to accept Puritan standards.

Religious freedom also did not exist in many of the southern colonies, although the Puritan church was not in control here. In Virginia, the Church of England, or the Anglican Church, became the official church of the colony. Attendance at Sunday church services was made compulsory

and anyone who broke the Sabbath could be arrested as a criminal. Until the mid-18th century Virginia's laws successfully prevented the growth of rival churches.

The Church of England was also the official church in North Carolina, South Carolina, and Georgia. The citizens of these southern colonies—even non-Anglicans—were forced to pay a tax for the salaries of Anglican ministers. This policy created resentment, but the practice continued until the Revolutionary War.

Various governors and ministers attempted to make the Church of England the official church of New York. Lord Cornbury, governor of

▼ *Massachusetts, 1651. Obadiah Holmes, a member of the newly formed Baptist Church, is whipped by intolerant Puritans.*

New York from 1702 to 1708, arrested numerous non-Anglican preachers for speaking in public. He also petitioned the colony's assembly to sponsor Anglicanism. While Cornbury succeeded in discouraging some non-Anglicans from practicing their beliefs, he failed to persuade the New York Assembly to officially sanction the Church of England. Strong ties between church and state also existed in the Spanish and French colonial territories. In these areas the government-sponsored Roman Catholic Church dominated the religious scene, and other denominations rarely existed. Catholic bishops and royal governors often worked together to maintain order. This partnership only served to increase the influence of the church and the crown.

FREE AT LAST

While most of colonial America did not experience religious freedom, some important movements toward toleration did exist. In Massachusetts a minister named Roger Williams challenged Puritan dominance. Williams felt that governmental interference with religion could only harm true spiritual feeling. His views upset the leadership of Massachusetts, and in 1635 these leaders banished

▲ *Bruton Parish Church in Williamsburg, Virginia, where religious freedom became protected by law in 1785.*

◄ *In 1770 rumors began to circulate in New England that the British were about to appoint a Church of England bishop for the colonies. This cartoon portrays the reaction of the settlers.*

Williams from the colony. The next year Williams founded the city of Providence in what would become Rhode Island. This colony established no church and allowed freedom of worship. Rhode Island's religious toleration attracted many persecuted groups, including Quakers, Baptists, and Jews. Throughout the colonial period Rhode Island's policies served as a rare example of an open-minded attitude to religion.

Another important step occurred in 1649. In that year Maryland passed the Act of Toleration, which protected the religious preferences of various groups, although only Christians. For the next four decades Maryland became a center for many persecuted people, especially Roman Catholics. Then the Church of England became the official church in Maryland. After the establishment of Anglicanism Maryland officials ignored the Act of Toleration. Although the act was no longer effective, it did set an example for later generations to follow.

William Penn, the founder of Pennsylvania, also promoted religious freedom in his colony. Although he required that all of the colony's citizens believe in God, he did not force any particular beliefs on the people. This encouraged large numbers of Moravians, Church of the Brethren, and Mennonites to settle in the region. Pennsylvania was also one of the few British colonies that allowed Roman Catholics to worship freely and publicly.

RELIGION AND THE REVOLUTION

In the mid-18th century two important movements were formed that led to greater religious toleration. The Great Awakening, with its revival of crusading, emotional religion, had a revolutionary effect on all the major churches. New England's governments attempted to control the Awakening by threatening to ban its leaders, but their attempts met with little success. New ideas of the time, which viewed governmental control of religion as an attack on human rights, also helped diminish the influence of the New England governments. Prominent thinkers such as Thomas Jefferson and James Madison supported this new viewpoint. These men promoted religious freedom in Virginia, and by 1785 Jefferson's Virginia Act for Establishing Religious Freedom became law.

By the time of the Revolutionary War religious freedom had slowly increased. Many Revolutionary leaders began to challenge the idea of an established, state-sponsored church. Although these leaders felt religion was vital to society's moral well-being, they did not believe that the government should uphold one denomination as the official church of the state. These sentiments blossomed at the Constitutional Convention.

After the adoption of the Federal Constitution, James Madison and other national leaders prepared 10 amendments. These amendments, known as the Bill of Rights, attempted to limit governmental control over a citizen's life. The First Amendment stated that the national government could not promote an established church, although individual states could still do so. This amendment gave American citizens the right to worship without interference from the federal government.

SEE ALSO

CONSTITUTIONAL CONVENTION
- EDWARDS, JONATHAN ■ GREAT AWAKENING
- JEFFERSON, THOMAS ■ MASSACHUSETTS
- MAYFLOWER ■ NEW ENGLAND
- PENN, WILLIAM ■ PENNSYLVANIA ■ RELIGION
- RHODE ISLAND

▼ *Modern-day Mennonites still live much as their ancestors did when they migrated from Germany to North America in the 17th century. In 1683 William Penn granted land in Pennsylvania to 18 Mennonite families. The religious tolerance they found here encouraged many more to leave Europe forever.*

CLOTHING

The clothes worn in the colonies were as varied as the people that wore them. Because the settlers came from many countries and all kinds of backgrounds, they wore different types of clothing according to their nationality, wealth, profession, and even religion. At first styles were simply a reflection of European fashions, since people brought with them the clothes they had worn in their homeland. In some cases they continued to wear them for many generations—the Germans of Pennsylvania and the Dutch of New York state, for example, were often seen wearing traditional outfits up to the time of the Revolution. In general, however, a colonial style developed over the years to suit the new environment and way of life.

KEEPING IT SIMPLE

For the Pilgrim Fathers simplicity and modesty were an important part of their religious beliefs, and this was reflected in their clothes. They wore simple styles in plain, dark colors. Men and women wore steeple hats made from felt, although women sometimes covered their heads with bonnets or hoods. The Puritans of Massachusetts also dressed in a simple style, in dark colors such as russet, purple, and a shade of brown known as philly mort, which comes from the French words for dead leaf. They rarely wore black, however, since they believed it was not plain enough for ordinary people.

The leaders of the Massachusetts community even passed laws to control what people wore. In 1634, for example, a statute was passed to restrict the fashion for full sleeves that were slashed to reveal a luxurious

fabric beneath: it was forbidden to have more than one slash in each sleeve. Two years later the making or selling of fancy clothing such as lace was banned. Some people may have rebelled against the strict dress rules: wills have been found listing brightly colored undergarments that must have been worn in secret under their plain outer clothing.

FASHION STATEMENTS

As the church began to lose its influence and more people from different backgrounds arrived in the colonies, clothing styles became more varied. The major differences were linked to the wealth and profession of the wearer. In contrast to the Puritans,

▲ *The fashion among the upper classes of 17th-century Europe and America was for extravagant clothes in luxurious fabrics, designed to show off the wealth of the wearer.*

◄ Hats were always popular, although fashions changed over the years. This hatmaker is producing hats from felt, a fabric made by rolling and pressing wool fibers.

The settlers who made their living as craftsmen or merchants were often better off than similar classes in Europe and could afford better clothes. They were able to copy the fashions of the gentry and wore ruffled shirts, coats, buckled shoes, and cocked hats (hats with the large brim turned up). By the time of the Revolution farmers too were dressing in this way. The fashion at the end of the 18th century was to wear waistcoats and tight breeches fastened at the knee with buttons and buckles.

CLOTHES FOR WORKING

Workers in the fields wore much more practical clothing, usually long trousers or breeches, a smock or a coarse, linen shirt that reached to the knees, a felt hat, and leather shoes, either with laces or, for the better off, with buckles.

Women, whether in a town or the country, wore a tight-fitting bodice and a full skirt over which was an apron. A fine piece of white cotton,

the wealthy plantation owners continued to dress in the elaborate styles popular throughout 17th-century Europe. Both men and women wore luxurious fabrics such as velvet, satin, and silk, and their clothes were decorated with lace, embroidery, and ribbons, all designed to show off the wealth of the owner. Ladies' skirts were very full, with hooped petticoats beneath. They wore dainty, high-heeled shoes, fastened with ribbons or buckles. Men's shoes were made of leather and fastened with a gold or silver buckle, often covered with jewels. Clothes such as these, or the fabric to make them, were sent from Europe, usually England or France.

SPANISH STYLE

The upper-class Spanish believed that a person's appearance and clothing revealed their status and distinguished them from the natives and other Spaniards. Even in the heat of New Spain they went to great lengths to wear the fancy clothes of their home country. Valuable clothes were carefully looked after and passed on to the next generation: fashions were therefore very slow to change.

▶ Wigs became fashionable in the second half of the 17th century, and different styles were worn by men of all classes. The more elaborate wigs were long and curled, and dusted with white powder.

C

▶ *A Quaker of the late 18th century. Beneath his frock coat he is wearing knee-length breeches and white stockings.*

called a kerchief, was often worn to cover the shoulders and chest and tucked into the top of the bodice. A woman's head was usually covered, with either a mobcap, a bonnet, a straw hat, or a felt hat similar to that worn by men. Settlers from France and Holland often wore wooden clogs on their feet.

WELL-DRESSED SERVANTS

Servants too had their own style of clothing, and like their employers', it varied according to their position. Those who worked for wealthy families were dressed in a uniform known as "livery," which was often very fancy, especially for servants such as footmen. Their outfits were highly decorated with braid, lace, and gilt buttons, and with their cocked hats they often looked like military uniforms. A servant's livery was designed around the colors of the family's coat of arms. George Washington's

servants, for instance, wore outfits in red and white. Servants in smaller households wore more simple clothes. Slaves were usually dressed in a cotton shirt, trousers, and a straw hat. They did not wear shoes.

In the backcountry European styles were not always practical for the settlers' new way of life, and many of

▼ *When working around the house, most women wore a mobcap to cover their hair, a bodice with a kerchief tucked inside, a heavy woolen skirt, and a large apron made of mattress ticking.*

those who came into contact with Native Americans adopted their more suitable clothes. Settlers often wore moccasins and, in winter, wrapped themselves in blankets. Hunters and trappers wore a tunic of coarse linen, often fringed, and protective leggings made of leather or fur and tied to the belt. On their heads were hats of coonskin, squirrel, or fox. Their leather belts were decorated with beads, and they kept their shot and knives in native pouches and sheaths.

HOME-MADE FABRICS

For the early settlers clothes were made from simple, coarse, homespun fabrics. Women who came to the colonies were skilled in spinning, weaving, and needlework and so made and repaired all the family's clothing. Clothes were made from whatever materials were available. In the early years colonists grew their own flax to make linen and kept sheep for their wool. Because of the large numbers of wild animals outfits made from leather and fur were much more common in the colonies than in Europe—they also provided warmth in the cold winters.

With the growth of trade across the Atlantic fine wools and other more luxurious fabrics were imported from Europe. Fabrics and ready-made clothes also became more easily available in towns. During the Revolutionary War English imports were restricted, and in the following years clothes and fashions were more frequently influenced by France.

▲ Frontiersmen dressed for tough backcountry conditions. Their coats were made of coarse linen, and their breeches or leggings were deerskin.

SEE ALSO

CRAFTS ■ MANUFACTURING ■ MASSACHUSETTS ■ RELIGION, PURITAN ■ RELIGION, QUAKER ■ WASHINGTON, GEORGE ■ WOMEN'S ROLES

C JEAN-BAPTISTE COLBERT

Jean-Baptiste Colbert, born in 1619, was controller of French government finances for 18 years, from 1665 until his death. He was also the minister for colonial affairs from 1663. He aimed to make his country, then ruled by Louis XIV, the most powerful nation in Europe. To help achieve this, he decided to change French policy in the colonies.

When Colbert took responsibility for the French colonies, the organization and administration of French settlements overseas were in the hands of a number of companies. The French government supplied them with funds and appointed their directors, but left them to conduct their own affairs more or less without further interference.

Colbert believed that French settlement should be more carefully planned, and the best way to do this

Colbert was an influential French aristocrat and proved to be a skilled colonial administrator.

▼ *Quebec grew and flourished under the policies adopted by Colbert.*

was to put it under central control. Adapting Spanish methods of rule, the French government took direct control of the administration of New France. The chief executive in the colony became a military governor appointed by Colbert. Control over the economy and taxation became the responsibility of a civil official known as the *intendant*.

Colbert also implemented a number of measures designed to increase the population of New France and secure his country's position there. He arranged for former soldiers of the French army to receive grants of land in the colonies if they wished to emigrate. Since there was a shortage of women and therefore families, French women willing to emigrate to Canada could take advantage of a free passage. Once there, the government would supply the new settlers with farming equipment, seeds, and farm animals, free of charge. The number of people living in Quebec increased rapidly, partly as a result of these measures.

After Colbert's death in 1683, however, the strong system of government he had built up began to lose its effect, as the attention of French rulers switched to a long succession of European wars.

SEE ALSO
■ GOVERNMENT, COLONIAL ■ NEW FRANCE
■ NEW SPAIN ■ QUEBEC CITY

CHRISTOPHER COLUMBUS

Christopher Columbus, the great mariner who opened a European window on the New World, was born in Genoa, Italy in 1451. Columbus was brought up in the weaving trade but opted for a life at sea. At the age of 25 his life took a dramatic turn when a Genoese merchant convoy he was sailing with on a commercial trip was attacked by French warships off the Portuguese coast. His ship was sunk, but Columbus managed to swim ashore and soon found himself in the busy port of Lisbon.

THE RICHES OF THE ORIENT

In the second half of the 15th century the people of Lisbon were gripped with "exploration fever." Portuguese sailors were leading the search to find a sea route to the Indies—the term Europeans then used to describe the region between India and Japan. The area was a great mystery to Europeans but known to contain fabulous wealth. Every year precious silks and gems, exotic spices, and perfumes trickled into Europe after being transported overland through Asia. These goods were very costly because of the difficulties of transporting them across such vast distances. European merchants had long been aware that it would be far less expensive, and quicker to transport the goods by boat, but no one had been able to find a safe sea route.

By the time Columbus arrived in Lisbon, the Portuguese were navigating further and further south along the coast of Africa in the correct belief that they would eventually reach the southern end of that continent and would then be able to sail east to the Indies. For unknown

reasons Columbus became fixated by an alternative strategy. It was accepted by educated people that the world was a sphere, so, in theory, by sailing west one would eventually arrive in the Indies. This was Columbus's great dream, and he spent years trying to get financial support for an expedition to prove it. A major obstacle was the fact that the most knowledgeable astronomers and navigators had calculated that Japan was far too

▼*Columbus's flagship, the* Santa Maria, *was originally a cargo vessel operated by a crew of 40 sailors.*

impoverished natives they encountered there bore little resemblance to the wealthy Orientals Columbus had expected, but he remained convinced that he had reached outlying islands of Japan or China. He spent the rest of 1492 in a fruitless search for the riches of the east in an area that would come to be called the West Indies. He set sail for home on January 3, 1493. On arriving in Spain, Columbus received a hero's welcome, and the Spanish court was fascinated by the natives, the parrots, and various artifacts he brought along as evidence of his amazing discovery.

Columbus made three more voyages to the Caribbean during his lifetime, persevering in his conviction that China was somewhere in the region. He died a disappointed man in 1506, never having discovered the route to the Orient. By this time, however, the Spanish had established a permanent foothold in the land they christened the "New World."

distant for ships of the time to sail there without stopping off for provisions. They were quite right about that, and Columbus was seriously wrong in his estimate that Japan was about as far to the west as in fact the Americas were.

MISTAKEN IDENTITY

Although King John of Portugal turned him down, Columbus finally persuaded Queen Isabella of Spain to provide the finances he needed for the voyage. On August 3 his three small ships, the *Santa Maria*, *Pinta*, and *Nina,* left port, reaching the Canary Islands after a week, where they stopped to make repairs. On September 6 the small fleet sailed southwest; the sailing conditions were perfect, and they made landfall in the Bahamas on October 12. The

▲ *Columbus's writings show that he was a devout Christian who saw his voyages as a means to finance a new Crusade to the Holy Land.*

▶ *A page from a 16th-century book, with Latin text, showing Columbus landing in the Bahamas. The actual island is not known for sure, but may have been San Salvador.*

SEE ALSO
SUGAR ■ TRADE ■ WEST INDIES

COMMITTEES OF CORRESPONDENCE

Committees of Correspondence played a major role in promoting colonial unity and in setting up the First Continental Congress of 1774. They were the focus of discontent and radical thought in the years before the American Revolution.

In June 1772 Governor Thomas Hutchinson announced that his salary would be paid by the British Crown rather than the people of Massachusetts. This was further evidence of Britain's determination to interfere with the colonists' affairs. In November 1772 Samuel Adams convinced the Boston town meeting to set up a "Committee of Correspondence" to issue a letter "to state the Rights of the Colonists and of this Province in particular," and to send a copy to every town in Massachusetts. Most of the towns replied, and 80 of them had formed their own Committees of Correspondence by February 1773.

THE SEEDS OF REVOLUTION

In March the Virginia Assembly formed a similar committee, with members such as Patrick Henry and Thomas Jefferson, to encourage cooperation between the colonies. Other colonies followed suit and soon an information network had been set up. These committees exchanged ideas and information on behalf of the colonial assemblies, the town meetings, and the Sons of Liberty (a secret society opposed to British taxation). They helped people keep abreast of events and coordinated resistance to British government.

Though the committees had no legal standing, they did have the power of persuasion on their side and a great deal of popular support. Their success led one Loyalist to call them "the foulest, subtlest, and most venomous serpent ever issued from the egg of sedition."

SEE ALSO

ADAMS, SAMUEL ■ CONTINENTAL CONGRESS ■ HENRY, PATRICK ■ JEFFERSON, THOMAS ■ SONS OF LIBERTY

▼ *Samuel Adams was the first colonial politician to propose the Committees of Correspondence. Throughout his political career he played a crucial role in the fight against Parliament's interference in the colonies.*

CONNECTICUT

Connecticut was one of the 13 colonies established during the early settlement of America. The frontiers of the colony formed a rectangular shape within the southern part of New England. The land was densely forested, with swampy flood plains and tidal marshes.

The original inhabitants of the region were Algonquian Native Americans, scattered across the land in some 16 separate tribes, and with a population of between 5,000 and 7,000. The name Connecticut comes from the Algonquian word for the Connecticut River, *Quinnetukut*, which means "the long river whose waters are driven by wind and tide."

In the early 17th century European explorers began to penetrate the continent and make contact with the Native Americans. Dutchman Adriaen Block navigated the Connecticut River from 1614. Sailing in a shallow-bottomed boat and anchoring at sites such as Suckiaug village (near the site of Hartford), he traded in furs with the local natives.

THE FUR TRADE TAKES OFF

Stories of the abundant resources to be found in Connecticut reached the port of New Amsterdam, and traders eager to exploit the region ventured into the wilderness. Dutch fur-trading posts were established on the sites of Saybrook Point and Hartford. Other trading sites soon appeared along the river as English settlers from the Plymouth colony followed the Dutch.

▼ *In 1685 James II sent Governor Andros to Connecticut to cancel its royal charter and so increase English control of the colony. During the handing-over ceremony the charter mysteriously disappeared.*

The first Europeans to establish permanent settlements in Connecticut came from the Massachusetts Bay Colony, which was inhabited mainly by Puritan settlers, the first of whom had left England in 1630. The political independence they achieved in Massachusetts, coupled with their strong beliefs, was used to create a strict religious community there.

Some members of the community, however, felt that the demands for strict conformity to Puritan teaching were as oppressive as the religious laws they had sought to escape in England. Non-Puritan groups such as Quakers, and outspoken individuals such as Ann Hutchinson, who publicly disagreed with some of the beliefs of the Puritan church, were not tolerated and often faced punishment for their refusal to toe the line. The Reverend Thomas Hooker became the leader of a group of people who decided to leave Massachusetts.

They began to travel south in search of new land and greater religious freedom, venturing along the coast and into the Connecticut valley. By 1636 settlers had founded the first three towns by the Connecticut River—Hartford, Wethersfield, and Windsor—all of which took their names from English towns.

A LOCAL CONSTITUTION

It was the political organization of these towns that eventually earned Connecticut its nickname "The Constitution State." In 1639, under the leadership of Reverend Hooker, the three towns united to form the Hartford Colony and created the Fundamental Orders of Connecticut as their basis for government. This closely followed the example of Massachusetts Bay, which was a self-governing community largely free of royal interference from England. This formal agreement created an annual

▲ *The Connecticut River, flowing through an area of dense forests, was one of the few rivers in the colony that were suitable for boats.*

C

assembly of law-makers and provided for the election of a governor. It was a major step in the political development of the colony. The orders were then followed by a royal charter from King Charles II in 1662. The charter increased the independence of the colony and placed its government firmly in the hands of the property owners of the territory. It also absorbed two other colonies into Connecticut—New Haven and Rhode Island, although the merger with Rhode Island lasted only for a year as it received its own charter in 1663.

MYSTERIOUS DISAPPEARANCE
The successor to Charles II, James II, sought to reduce the freedoms enjoyed by the settlers and sent Governor Andros to Connecticut in 1685 with orders to cancel the charter. In a mysterious incident during a formal ceremony to hand over the charter, the candles blew out, and the document disappeared. There is a legend that a Captain Joseph Wadsworth snatched the document

▼ Before it was colonized, the southern parts of Connecticut were covered in thick oak forests, which provided valuable timber for the construction of houses and boats. Even today, much of the state is still densely forested.

and hid it in a hollow oak tree, later called the Charter Oak. The rights of the colony were restored in 1690, when the Attorney General decided the 1662 Charter was still in force.

HOSTILITIES BEGIN
Relations between the Native Americans and the first European explorers in Connecticut had been good. But the first traders and fishermen who came to the land had brought diseases with them, and the Native Americans were suffering greatly by the time the first Puritans arrived. The cultural, economic, and religious differences between Native-American and settler communities eventually resulted in conflicts. In 1636, for example, a year after John Winthrop, Jr., was appointed the first governor of Connecticut, settlers became involved in a bitter war with

◄ Warriors from the Pequot tribes, from a coastal area east of the Connecticut River, waged war against the local white settlers. They raided villages and took captives as hostages.

▼ The First Church of Christ is one of the few remaining colonial buildings in Hartford, which is now the state's largest city.

The varied economy of Connecticut helped in its growth. Inland areas with good farmland and natural resources prospered; farmers raised cattle, pigs, and sheep, which they sold in the towns or exported. Coastal settlements such as New London and Mystic thrived on fishing and whaling. A coastline with a plentiful supply of timber close at hand meant that shipbuilding was also of great importance. The first American warship, the *Oliver Cromwell*, was built in the shipbuilding center of Essex in 1775. One of America's oldest colleges, Yale University, has its origins in Old Saybrook. The college was first opened for training church ministers in 1701 and later moved to New Haven in 1718.

SEE ALSO

ALGONQUIANS ■ HUTCHINSON, ANNE ■ KING PHILIP'S WAR ■ MASSACHUSETTS ■ RELIGION, PURITAN

the Pequot tribes. Settlers were murdered, tortured, and kidnapped, and in retaliation the Pequot village-fort of Mystic was attacked and many natives killed. Forty years later Connecticut suffered native attacks during King Philip's War of 1675–1678.

POPULATION BOOM

By 1636 there were 12,000 settlers living in settlements along the New England coastline and inland into Connecticut and New Hampshire (another refuge for those from Massachusetts). During the 17th and 18th centuries the population of Connecticut increased dramatically, swelled by births within the settler communities and also by groups of immigrants arriving directly from England. In 1720 the colony had a population of 60,000; in 1760 it had grown to 140,000.

CONSTITUTIONAL CONVENTION

The Constitutional Convention was a meeting to revise the Articles of Confederation, which had formed the constitution of the United States since 1781. Every state except Rhode Island sent delegates to the assembly, which was presided over by George Washington and held in Philadelphia's State House from May 25, 1787.

The problem with the Articles of Confederation was that the central government they created was not strong enough. There was general agreement on this issue, so it was decided to scrap the Articles altogether and devise a fresh constitution. The largest stumbling block to agreement was over the way the states would be represented in a new federal government. Many solutions were suggested. The Virginia Plan, put forward by Governor Edmund Randolph, called for two chambers of congress—an upper and a lower. The states would be represented in both according to population or wealth and by delegates who had been directly elected by the people.

A NORTH-SOUTH DIVIDE

This scheme appealed to Massachusetts, Pennsylvania, and other large states, but it was fiercely resisted by small states such as Delaware and New Jersey. They feared that it would give too much power to the larger states. William Paterson of New Jersey suggested another solution: keeping the existing single chamber with each state having equal representation.

This basic question was debated for a month, and it appeared that the convention would never reach agreement. Finally, a system that combined the two plans was proposed. The Great Compromise, as it was called, gave the states equal representation in an upper chamber, the Senate, and representation in a lower chamber, the House of

▲ *John Paul Jones, Benjamin Franklin, and George Washington at the Convention. Jefferson described it as "an assembly of demigods."*

Representatives, according to the size of the state's population. Once this was decided, the convention moved on to debate other pressing issues.

Slavery was not the controversial issue that it was to become in the 19th century, and although it already had many opponents, it was agreed that Congress would not interfere with the slave trade for 20 years.

It was in discussing representation that the slave trade became an important issue, and differences between the northern and the southern states soon became clear. An argument developed over whether slaves should be counted as part of a state's population. The southern states had large numbers of slaves, so it followed that if they were included in the population count, those states would have more representatives in the government. The northern states, meanwhile, had few slaves and argued not only that slaves should not count for representation but also that they should be viewed as property and therefore taxed. The Three-Fifths Compromise was eventually agreed: for both

▼ *In 1787 the Constitution bore the signatures of the delegates from 12 of the states. Formal approval from all of the states, however, was not achieved until May 1790.*

taxation and representation purposes a slave would be counted as three-fifths of a person.

AN INCREASE IN POWER

There was general agreement that the new government should have greater powers. It retained the right to declare war and peace and was granted the power to levy taxes and issue money, and to regulate trade between the states. The constitution was to be the supreme law of the land in all matters. The terms of office of the president and members were also worked out.

On September 17, 1787, the convention submitted the final wording of the new constitution to the old Congress. Although most of the delegates signed the document almost immediately, each state still had to ratify the constitution (give their formal approval). By July 1788, 11 of the 13 states had done this and the new government could begin to carry out its duties. North Carolina ratified in 1789, and Rhode Island in 1790.

SEE ALSO
ARTICLES OF CONFEDERATION ■ CONTINENTAL CONGRESS ■ SLAVE TRADE ■ SLAVERY ■ WASHINGTON, GEORGE

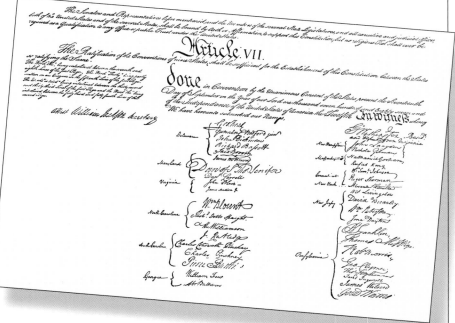

CONTINENTAL ARMY

The Continental Army existed for the duration of the Revolutionary War, during which time it evolved from an untrained rabble into an experienced and respected fighting force. When the delegates assembled in Philadelphia for the Second Continental Congress in May 1775, the events at Lexington and Concord just a few weeks before had made a war with Britain inevitable. One of the first acts of Congress was to call for the formation of a Continental Army to defend the colonies from the British.

A volunteer army of New Englanders had already formed from local militia units and was surrounding the garrison of British troops in Boston. Congress set about establishing supply lines to them and recruiting men from the southern colonies. George Washington, a Virginian who had distinguished himself in the French and Indian War, was appointed commander-in-chief. Thirteen generals were also appointed from all over the colonies; though some had been soldiers, most were chosen largely for political reasons.

A POPULAR CAUSE

Washington arrived in Cambridge, Massachusetts, to take up his command in July 1775. He found an eager but largely undisciplined band of volunteers who were committed to the pursuit of liberty but shared the Patriots' general mistrust of a standing (permanent) army. They regarded themselves as "citizen-soldiers," ready to disband as soon as the war was won, and as a result, most enlisted

▼ *Washington takes command of the army in July 1775. In reality, the soldiers were a far more untrained and dishevelled force than portrayed here. It was some time before all the troops were properly dressed and equipped.*

only for short periods—three or six months, a year at most. The assumption was that the volunteers would reenlist immediately if there was still a war to be won. But in reality many of them quit as soon as their time was up or took a few months off between enlistments to oversee their harvests. Desertion rates were high, around 20–25 percent, throughout the war.

RECRUITMENT DRIVE

By the end of the war a total of 220,000 free males aged between 16 and 45 had served in the army at some point. Recruitment was a constant problem, however, and there was a desperate shortage of volunteers and not enough trained or raw recruits to raise the army to the strength voted by Congress. Numbers had to be strengthened by state militias and volunteer irregulars. New methods were tried to boost recruitment and to persuade men to enlist for three years or for the duration of the war.

From 1777 each of the states was given a quota for men who had to enlist, mostly recruited with the offer of bounties of cash and land, sometimes supplied by Congress, sometimes by the states or towns.

▲ At the outbreak of war eager volunteers were quick to leave their homes and families to enlist. But when the enthusiasm wore off and the troops would no longer tolerate the bad conditions, there were numerous mutinies.

▶ Images of the Revolutionary War. Around the picture of Washington passing a section of troops are the flags, money, and weapons of the Revolution.

There was also a partial draft—a certain number of adult males in a state were ordered to enlist. But this was not easy to enforce, and often someone who was unwilling to fight would sponsor someone else to go to war in his place. This at least guaranteed the soldier's pay. Other enlisted men in the Continental Army were paid very little; their wives and families often suffered real hardship. Though the army was generally supplied by the states, support was not reliable, and soldiers often turned to impressment—simply taking what they needed—to get vital supplies.

In the opening months of the war discipline and organization in the Continental Army were poor. The volunteers were reluctant to accept orders without question and learned no drills. Each of the Continental regiments had its own uniform, but they were in short supply, and the men made do with what they had; militia uniforms, overalls, work shirts,

▲ *An American soldier primes his musket with gunpowder.*

diseases were common. More than 25,000 American troops died during the Revolutionary War; the most common cause was disease—10,000 lost their lives in this way.

VICTORIES AND DEFEATS

The bulk of Washington's army besieged Boston until March 1776, when the British garrison withdrew. This was hailed as a triumph, but other parts of the Continental Army were faring less well. A Canadian campaign, including an assault on Quebec led by Benedict Arnold, cost the army some 5,000 men between October 1775 and June 1776. The loss of Long Island and Manhattan created a mutual distrust between Washington and his troops. There were fewer than 3,000 troops remaining when they retreated across the Delaware in December 1776. Later that month at Trenton, and in January at Princeton, Washington achieved two small, but vital victories against the British.

In the fall of 1777 the army was defeated at the Battles of Brandywine and Germantown by British forces

rugs, and blankets were all called into service. Rich officers had theirs privately made. Because many of the soldiers considered laundry "women's work," they would wear the same clothes until they fell apart. Camps were equally neglected, and epidemic

---

EYEWITNESS

AT THE END OF 1779 WASHINGTON LED HIS MEN TO MORRISTOWN, NEW JERSEY. THAT WINTER WAS TO BE ONE OF THE COLDEST ON RECORD, AND HIS TROOPS SUFFERED GREAT HARDSHIPS. THIS IS THE ACCOUNT OF A PRIVATE MARTIN.

❝ *At one time it snowed the greater part of four days successively, and there fell nearly as many feet of snow and here was the keystone of the arch of starvation. We were absolutely, literally starved;—I do solemnly declare that I did not put a single morsel of Victuals [food] into my mouth for four days and as many nights, except a little black birch bark which I knawed off a stick of wood, if that can be called victuals. I saw several of the men roast their old shoes and eat them, and I was afterwards informed by one of the officers' waiters, that some of the officers killed and ate a favourite little dog that belonged to one of them.—If this was not 'suffering' I request to be informed what can pass under that name; if suffering like this did not 'try men's souls,' I confess that I do not know what could.* **❞**

◀ *Sharpshooter Tim Murphy snipes at British General Fraser during the Battle of Bemis Heights, New York, on October 7, 1777. Among the American troops were a number of very skilled marksmen.*

under General Howe, but at Saratoga it forced the British General Burgoyne to surrender his army.

In the winter of 1777–1778 the troops camped at Valley Forge. Though the men suffered cold and hunger, they had the opportunity to train properly. A Prussian general, Baron von Steuben, was given the post of drillmaster and taught the men the skills of battlefield maneuvers. The officers were given courses in tactics. Everyone was also lectured on the importance of camp hygiene in an effort to control the spread of disease.

The winter at Valley Forge considerably strengthened the Continental Army. Building on past experience, they avoided the pitched battles that suited their European foes and used their knowledge of the terrain to wear down an enemy weakened by the strain of fighting a war in unfamiliar country.

A TRIUMPHANT ARMY

At the end of the war, in 1783, Washington was at the head of a respected, professional, and disciplined army, but one that was soon to be disbanded, its work done. While often defeated in set-piece battles, the Continental Army had gained an overall victory over the British. It had symbolized the Patriots' cause and the new unity of the states. If the army had not survived and had left only the state militias to fight for the freedom of the American people, the Revolutionary cause would almost certainly have collapsed.

SEE ALSO

AMERICAN REVOLUTIONARY WAR
▪ CONTINENTAL CONGRESS ▪ CORNWALLIS, LORD CHARLES ▪ LEXINGTON AND CONCORD ▪ TRENTON, BATTLE OF ▪ VALLEY FORGE ▪ WASHINGTON, GEORGE ▪ YORKTOWN, BATTLE OF

▼ *The victorious Continental Army, led by George Washington, marches into New York in November 1783 as the British evacuate.*

CONTINENTAL CONGRESS

The First Continental Congress was held on September 5, 1774, to discuss the British Intolerable Acts. These were a series of repressive measures imposed on Massachusetts by the British Parliament in retaliation for the Boston Tea Party in 1773. The intent was to isolate Massachusetts from the other colonies, but the result was the direct opposite. The colonies were outraged by the measures, and in September 1775 delegates from all the colonies except Georgia traveled to Carpenters' Hall, Philadelphia, to decide on a united response.

The declaration of personal rights that Congress made was later reflected in the Declaration of Independence. It also demanded an end to taxation without representation (the colonists resented paying taxes to a government in London in which they had no involvement) and objected to the British keeping troops in the colonies without their consent. Then, to step up the pressure, Congress petitioned King George, listing 13 acts of parliament passed since 1763 that were harmful to American rights. Finally, to give teeth to its demands, Congress declared a trade boycott with Great Britain. On October 26, 1774, Congress adjourned, having agreed that a second congress should be convened the following March, to judge Britain's response.

A TIMELY MEETING

The Second Continental Congress (with Georgia now in attendance) met on May 10, 1775, again at Philadelphia, this time in the State House. The situation was dramatically different. Three weeks earlier serious

▼ *Congressmen cast their votes for Independence in the same hall where, two years previously, they had first met.*

▲ *Carpenters' Hall in Philadelphia, the site of the first Continental Congress.*

why the Americans demanded independence from Britain. At the same time, Congress appointed a committee to devise a constitution for the nation they were now fighting to create. This constitution, the Articles of Confederation, was finally adopted in 1781 and remained in effect until it was replaced by the Federal Constitution of 1787.

Continental congresses continued to meet as the American army fought its way to victory. In 1787, however, it was clear to many that the Articles of Confederation were not effective, and a new framework for government was needed. Congress responded to this need by calling a Constitutional Convention in May 1787.

SEE ALSO

ARTICLES OF CONFEDERATION ■ BOSTON ■ BOSTON TEA PARTY ■ CONSTITUTIONAL CONVENTION ■ DECLARATION OF INDEPENDENCE ■ GEORGE III ■ INTOLERABLE ACTS ■ LEXINGTON AND CONCORD ■ WASHINGTON, GEORGE

fighting had occurred at Lexington and Concord, and as Congress met, the British garrison at Boston was under siege.

Congress immediately announced the creation of an American army commanded by George Washington. At the same time, on July 5, 1775, it sent one more petition to the English king in an attempt to avoid war. The "Olive Branch" petition put the blame for the situation on the British parliament, not the king, but King George refused to accept the petition.

By this time Congress had gradually assumed more and more power and on July 2, 1776, it took the decisive step of cutting all ties with Great Britain. Two days later Congress approved the Declaration of Independence, which explained

▶ *King George issued a royal proclamation declaring the colonists to be in a state of rebellion.*

By the KING,

A PROCLAMATION,

For suppressing Rebellion and Sedition.

GEORGE R.

God save the King.

LONDON

Printed by Charles Eyre and William Straban, Printers to the King's most Excellent Majesty. 1775.

C LORD CORNWALLIS

Charles, Lord Cornwallis was a distinguished British general and statesman who is chiefly remembered for one shattering setback in an otherwise successful career. He was forced to surrender to combined American and French forces at Yorktown, Virginia, on October 19, 1781. This defeat effectively ended the Revolutionary War.

The eldest son of an earl, Lord Cornwallis arrived in America in 1776 with the rank of major general. He served under Sir William Howe during the successful British campaign in New York and New Jersey that fall and at the Battle of Brandywine Creek in September 1777. In 1778 General Sir Henry Clinton took over from Howe as overall commander of British forces in North America, and Cornwallis was appointed his second-in-command.

After a successful siege of Charleston, South Carolina, in May 1780 Clinton returned to his headquarters in New York City. For the remainder of the war the conduct of the British campaign in the south was left to Cornwallis.

NO WAY OUT

Cornwallis began well enough, defeating an American army at Camden, South Carolina, in August 1780. But in January 1781 at Cowpens, South Carolina, he was heavily defeated by a new army under the command of General Nathanael Greene. The prolonged, seesaw nature of this struggle for the Carolinas depleted Cornwallis's forces, and by August 1781 he had moved his army to the Yorktown peninsula to await reinforcements from a British fleet. By the time the British fleet arrived, an even greater French fleet was in position to block it. Then in a brilliant pincer movement Washington cornered Cornwallis and his men with a vastly superior American-French army. Cornwallis had no choice but to surrender.

The defeated general went on to become Governor General of India in 1786 and Viceroy of Ireland in 1798. He died in 1805.

▼ *Cornwallis surrenders to the American army. Surrounded at sea and on land, he was left with no alternative.*

SEE ALSO

AMERICAN REVOLUTIONARY WAR ■ GREENE, NATHANAEL ■ YORKTOWN, BATTLE OF

FRANCISCO DE CORONADO

Francisco Vazquez de Coronado was the leader of a long, exhausting, and ultimately disappointing Spanish expedition into the American southwest between 1540 and 1542. Born in 1510 in Spain, he left his home in Salamanca to make his fortune in New Spain (Mexico) in 1535. Coronado quickly gained favor with the viceroy and was appointed governor of the western province of Nueva Galicia. There were rumors in the province of fabulously wealthy native Zuni communities that lived on the border of present-day New Mexico and Arizona. Coronado was put in charge of an expedition to conquer these so-called "Seven Cities of Cibola," and in 1540, together with

▲ *Despite the vast distance that Coronado and his men had traveled, his expedition into the southwest was judged a failure.*

300 Spanish adventurers and 1,000 native allies, he set out on his quest from Nueva Galicia.

The expedition reached its goal in July 1540 to find that the reports were completely bogus and that Cibola was just a humble village of perhaps a hundred families. The Spanish duly conquered it and then dispersed in several parties to search for the elusive riches. They found none. Those who traveled west sighted the Grand Canyon. Those heading east found numerous Pueblo communities settled along the Rio Grande. Coronado set up headquarters near present-day Albuquerque, New Mexico.

During the winter of 1540–1541 his men violently suppressed the Pueblos before setting off in the spring in response to rumors of yet another fabulous land called Quivira. The expedition crossed Texas and Oklahoma before reaching a nondescript Wichita village in central Kansas—the supposed kingdom of Quivira. A disheartened Coronado led his weary expedition back to New Spain, reaching Nueva Galicia in 1542. He was stripped of his governorship in 1545 and died in 1554.

◄ *Part of Coronado's expedition headed off to the west and were the first Europeans to see the Grand Canyon.*

SEE ALSO

NEW SPAIN ■ PUEBLO

C COUREURS DE BOIS

The *coureurs de bois* (French for "runners of the woods") were unlicensed fur traders operating out of the French colony of New France. The fur trade was the main source of income in New France; indeed, the colony existed mainly to satisfy the constant demand in Europe for the exotic beaver, otter, deer, fox, and muskrat skins to be found in colonial America. The animals were caught by native trappers who then sold the skins or bartered them in exchange for goods.

To keep control of trade in the valuable pelts (animal skins) and to keep French settlers in agricultural communities along the St. Lawrence River rather than scattered through the

▶ *The French traders traveled far into the backcountry and dressed to cope with the climate and environment. Their clothes were mainly made from skins, their hats from fur.*

▼ *The traders' livelihood depended on good relations with the natives.*

backcountry, the French government only issued a limited number of licenses to traders. This created a class of unlicensed traders called *coureurs de bois* who ignored the law and traded illegally with the Native Americans. Bypassing the forts and trading posts that had been set up to receive the furs, they voyaged deep into native territory to get the pelts before the licensed traders could.

By the early 18th century around 800 *coureurs de bois* were active in the New World, operating in groups of between 10 and 20 men. While the

C

coureurs de bois traded regularly with Native-American communities around the Great Lakes and the Mississippi Valley, some of them penetrated as far west as present-day Saskatchewan in the north and Santa Fe in the south.

Part of the reason for the government's attempts to license the fur trade was to control the kind and quantity of goods that were used in exchange with the Native Americans. Initially European traders offered items that had ritual significance for the natives, such as beads, or practical metal goods, such as hatchets, knives, kettles, and needles. They were given the valuable skins in return. As these goods became more common, traders tried to entice the Indians with luxury items such as cloth and mirrors. But as the Native Americans had increasing contact with Europeans, they soon began to want the guns and alcohol that the French traders carried. In the desperate race to get the furs unscrupulous traders were happy to supply these European commodities, both of which were destructive in their own way and had a devastating effect on native lives and culture.

LIVING WITH THE LOCALS

To help them communicate with the native people, the *coureurs de bois* often learned their languages. They also took Native-American wives and lived in their communities. However, many of them also had French wives in the settler communities, but since many Native-American tribes practiced polygamy (whereby a person can have more than one partner at the same time), they did not object.

Generally speaking, native peoples had good relations with the French, who were more interested in acquiring furs than in colonizing the territory or clearing the land. The French church was eager to convert Native Americans to Christian beliefs, and from experiences elsewhere, French officials often encouraged marriage between French men and Native-American women: France had managed to establish a prosperous timber trade in Brazil partly because of intermarrying.

Although the offspring of the inter-racial marriages so common among the *coureurs de bois* were sometimes referred to as metis ("mixed") they usually lived as full-blooded natives in their mothers' tribes. The metis are still recognized in Canada as a distinct population group.

SEE ALSO

FUR TRADE ■ METIS AND MESTIZOS ■ NEW FRANCE

▼ Coureurs de bois *in the streets of 18th-century Quebec. Once they had traded with the Native Americans, they would return to towns such as this to sell the skins and furs at great profit.*

C CRAFTS

The production of crafts and handiwork within the American colonies took a long time to flourish. For much of the 17th century colonists imported almost all of their furnishings, tools, books, and even wooden tableware, such as bowls and plates, from England and the rest of Europe. From the earliest days of settlement there were craftsmen in the colonies, although they made up only a small proportion of the population. They brought with them the skills and techniques they had learned in Europe, and as a consequence the styles and trends of pieces created in America naturally showed European influences.

TEXTILES

The production of textiles and textile goods was of great importance in the colonies, particularly in rural areas. Spinning, weaving, and sewing were

▼ *Part of a sampler embroidered by a New Hampshire woman. The bird and flowers are typical of the designs used to decorate colonial handiworks.*

usually referred to as cottage industries because they took place in the home rather than in a shop or factory. Nonetheless, many of these products, especially woven cloth, were shipped elsewhere and sold. Although early in the colonial period most professional weavers were male, many historians believe that farmwives learned the craft of weaving from itinerant weavers (who moved from one place to another to work), because the trade had become the domain of women by the end of the colonial period. Women produced coverlets, blankets, and rugs for household use and for sale to friends and neighbors.

Many young women embroidered samplers (pieces of decorative needlework) that featured the alphabet and numbers. These were a means of learning different stitches as well as practicing lettering. Fancy needlework was considered the mark of a gentlewoman—one who did not engage in hard labor from dawn to dusk and who had some spare time on her hands. Teaching the art of fine needlework to women at finishing schools was popular in the 1700s.

Starting in 1731, Martha Gazley advertized her needlework school in the New York newspapers on a regular basis.

POTTERY

The clay deposits that can be excavated from many parts of North America supported a number of crafts. Clay was turned into bricks and roof tiles for homes, and pots and plates for cooking and eating. Bricks were first made in Virginia in 1612 and in New England in 1641. Pottery production began almost as early. John Pride of Salem, Massachusetts, began in 1641, and by 1690 there was at least one man in Philadelphia who produced pots and clay tobacco pipes. There were also a number of Dutch potters practicing in 17th-century Manhattan.

Another type of pottery began to appear in late 17th-century America. Archeologists are beginning to recognize fragments of Native-American and African-American pottery, known as colonoware, at sites associated with these people. Unlike European pottery, which is shaped on a turning wheel, this pottery is created with coils of clay. Colonoware vessels were used for everyday purposes such as cooking and food storage.

In the 18th century German immigrants from the Rhine Valley brought another type of pottery to America. Their fancy earthenware, a reddish-colored type of pottery baked at low temperatures, and their gray and blue stoneware, fired at higher temperatures to make it harder and more durable, reflected Old World designs and techniques. Potters in eastern Pennsylvania, western Virginia, and North Carolina produced hundreds of examples of earthenware and stoneware in the 18th century. Many potters were farmers who turned to pottery work as a side business during the winter months. In some instances the potter's wife or children added the decoration to the clay pieces.

Although these pieces were meant to be useful rather than simply decorative, they often included extra, individual artistic touches. The red, brown, or buff-colored glaze was supplemented with decorations added by pouring a watery yellow, green, blue, or pink clay mixture (called slip) through a quill and onto the plate, much as a cake is decorated today. Pictures of tulips, birds, or people were drawn with lines of slip. Cookware and serving dishes, were decorated in this manner. Stoneware, like crocks and jugs, was usually glazed in gray or brown.

▲ *The interior of an 18th-century potters' workshop. On the right-hand side a potter is "throwing" a lump of clay on a foot-powered wheel. In front of him another worker is trimming a thrown pot on an upturned barrel.*

▶ *A pottery switchel bottle decorated with a swirling glaze. Switchel was a nonalcoholic drink made from sugar, ginger, molasses, vinegar, and water.*

◄ *This woman is skeining (looping) wool. The wool is being wound directly from the spinning wheel (where the wool fibers are twisted into yarn) onto the large skeining frame to the right of the picture.*

WOODWORK

Another necessary item that could be as simple or as elaborate as the user demanded was household furniture. Craftsmen who built furniture were called joiners (because they joined pieces of wood), turners (these were the people who actually turned a piece of wood on a foot-powered lathe to make it round), or cabinetmakers. In 17th-century Virginia, Maryland, and the Carolinas almost all furniture was imported, while the same was true for much of New York and Pennsylvania. In New England, however, cabinetmakers created simple furniture as well as high-style pieces throughout the 1600s. By 1642 there were more than 50 turners and joiners in Boston. Their furniture was custom produced to order, rather than mass-produced.

By the 18th-century colonial cabinetmakers were producing work

▶ *A chair frame spinning wheel of the type used in 18th-century Connecticut for spinning flax. The wheel was operated by the two pedals at the bottom, and the flax was kept wet by water dripping from the gourd mounted above the upper wheel.*

comparable to the best in England. For the most part they reproduced designs that were popular in Great Britain. One exception was the 18th-century German cabinetmakers in Pennsylvania, western Maryland, and Virginia. They made colorful painted chests and schranks (big wooden closets that resembled those found in the Rhine Valley region of Europe). Dower chests, trunks filled with household items like sheets and clothing for a new bride, were extremely popular. The artwork, in bright greens, reds, blues, and yellows, often included tulips, birds, and the year.

METALWORK
German craftsmen shone in other areas as well. The Conestoga freight wagons they made were decorated with fancy ironwork that often incorporated the same tulip pattern. Ironworkers also made weathervanes, hinges, laundry irons, and tools that often reflected an artistic touch in addition to the practical value of the item. The long rifles that helped defend the 18th-century American frontier, later known as Kentucky long rifles, were the creation of German gunsmiths. Carvings on the gun stocks and fancy metalwork were often used to decorate these rifles. German artistry was even reflected in the ironmaking industry. Square and rectangular stoveplates, measuring several feet on each side and up to half an inch thick, were used to create a box stove or to put in the back of a fireplace to reflect heat into the room. Although a flat surface on these plates worked just as well as a fancy one with a raised design, many ironworkers took the time to add a

▲ *A Conestoga wagon of the type first made in the Conestoga Valley, Lancaster County, Pennsylvania, during the 18th century. Originally built for hauling freight and farm produce, the Conestoga wagon was strong, reliable, and easy to maintain. In the 19th century Conestoga wagons became popular with pioneers heading west.*

C

personal touch. Depicted on the stoveplate surface were names and dates, the trademark tulip, and scenes from the Bible.

Braziers and tinsmiths—who work in brass and tin—also found a market for their wares. Their products included buckles for belts, shoes, and harnesses, nails, buttons, clock parts, and even pins. Thin brass wire was dipped into molten tin to make pins, which were in great demand for dressmaking.

The availability of professional tradesmen and craftsmen in New England towns meant that people were not forced to make or to buy their handicrafts from Europe. The thriving commercial center of Boston, for example, had a variety of crafts and tradespeople very early. There was a great demand in colonial

▶ *A quilting bee was an occasion when friends and neighbors got together and shared their needlework skills.*

▼ *A piece of Stiegel-type glassware engraved with a tulip design. Although Stiegel's own factory failed, glassware in his distinctive style continued to be produced.*

Boston for silverware, in particular the bowls and tea services produced by exiled French Huguenots.

One Huguenot silversmith who set up business in the city was Apollos De Revire. He passed on his skills to his son Paul Revere, who became an important figure in the American Revolution and designed a popular silver bowl that is still made today. It is called a Revere bowl in his honor.

GLASSWARE

Many of the skilled craftsmen catered mainly to the upper classes, providing furnishings that spoke of elegance and sophistication rather than simple usefulness.

Henry William Stiegel was a German ironworker who came to America in 1750. After making money in iron, he sank everything into a glassworks in Manheim, Pennsylvania. Before Stiegel's efforts most glass production in America consisted of turning out crude, dark green bottle

glass or coarse window glass filled with bubbles. Stiegel, nicknamed "Baron" for his extravagant living, employed as many as 130 highly skilled men in 1773. They produced clear glass tumblers, decanters, wine glasses, and cruets (salt, pepper, and mustard pots). Although Stiegel's glassworks represented the pinnacle of glass craftsmanship in colonial America, he went bankrupt in 1774 when his taste for fine living caught up with him.

Crafts and handiworks were a part of the American colonies from the beginning but did not blossom fully until the 18th century. By the end of the colonial period Americans had taken the skills and techniques brought from Europe and created a brand of artistry and skill that was uniquely American.

SEE ALSO

CLOTHING ▪ FAMILY LIFE ▪ FURNITURE ▪ MANUFACTURING ▪ WOMEN'S ROLES

The women of the colonies took great pride in their appliqué quilts. Quilting, or the technique of sewing together two layers of cloth with a heavy, insulating filling in the middle, dates back to medieval times. In Europe quilted underclothing provided warmth for women and served as protection under knights' armor. However, the idea of creating quilted bedcovers was something that arose in the colonies, perhaps because of the long, cold winters. The women who made these quilts added very fancy touches and designs. The quilts were sometimes stitched at a quilting bee, a gathering of women who came together to work and socialize.

CRIME AND PUNISHMENT

Although the first settlers to arrive in North America from England were eager to build a new country, they brought many aspects of the English way of life with them. One of these was common law.

Common law originated under the Tudors, who ruled England between 1485 and 1603. The monarchs appointed aristocratic family friends and associates as justices of the peace. These officials traveled out to the rural counties three or four times a year to arrange assize courts, where local criminals were tried and, if found guilty, sentenced. The assize courts were often held in public places, such as local taverns and inns.

The justices tried to apply the same laws and sentences to similar cases. This principle was applied across the whole range of offenses, laying the foundations for a uniform system of law in England.

LAWS AND LAWYERS

English settlers in America remained subject to the laws of England until the Declaration of Independence in 1776. Since most early expeditions were organized by small companies funded by stockholders, the stockholders expected to have some legal control over the new territories to ensure that their investments were secure. In 1609 the Virginia Charter gave total control over the colony to a council based in London. Virginia governor Sir Thomas Gates drafted a code of laws in 1611 that, although harsh, instilled a discipline that helped the colonists survive in the difficult

environment. The laws required all colonists to attend church on a daily basis and imposed heavy penalties for crimes against the Virginia Company, which owned the colony. Many crimes were punishable by death.

Some early colonists had studied law and so were familiar with the system of common law. Unfortunately, their knowledge tended to die with them since no law schools were established in the colonies until the 18th century. Because there were no full-time lawyers in the colonies in the 1600s, respected members of the community, known as "lay persons," dealt with legal matters on a part-time basis. Since they were untrained, the influence of English law—which formed the basis of the colonial legal system—began to decrease.

In the 1720s in New York there were only six practicing lawyers. By the mid-1700s the number of lawyers had increased, and they had begun to organize themselves. Although lawyers were more numerous, the need for them still far outweighed their numbers.

Each colony had its own distinct way of administering the law,

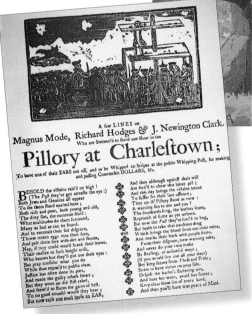

Even as late a 1767, when this poster was printed, criminals such as these money forgers were publicly punished.

There was a set of stocks in most village or town centers, and it was used as a punishment for minor offenses. Like these two unfortunate drunks, who have woken up with more than a headache to contend with, offenders would be locked in and forced to suffer verbal abuse from their fellow villagers. They were also pelted with rotten food and mud.

influenced by the beliefs and attitudes of the population. Added to this was the fact that the colonies were settled at different times, and their laws varied accordingly. The earliest settlers favored laws that punished those who offended their religious beliefs and laws that preserved their own faith against interference from other religions. In areas that had a strong French or Spanish influence, however—Quebec, California, Texas, and the Mississippi Valley—the legal system generally reflected that of the parent country, where Catholicism was the national religion.

The Pilgrim Fathers who traveled to America on the *Mayflower* were extremely strict in applying religious laws. In 1628 they used a force of militiamen to expel a group of colonists who had not shown proper Puritan devotion to God. Crimes that went against the Ten Commandments were punished severely, but the way that offenders were tried varied greatly. In Massachusetts there were a variety of courthouses in which offenses were heard, yet in Virginia all cases were tried in a single central court in Williamsburg.

English settlers in every colony were quick to establish county courts through which justices of the peace could prosecute trials for minor offenses. They also created district

C courts to try more serious offenses and a supreme court—often presided over by the governor's council—for crimes of treason and mutiny. It was very unusual for the settlers to carry out trial and sentencing without employing lawyers or judges. Although only the settlers of Rhode Island copied the English legal system exactly, similarities to the English courts remained evident in colonial America, even in the more independent colonies.

LAW ENFORCEMENT

Because there was no colonial police force, it was usually left to the public to catch criminals. The offender would be chased down and apprehended by a group of townsfolk, and then locked up until the trial could be arranged. Cruel physical punishments were often inflicted on offenders, and virtually all settlements had a set of stocks in the center.

Public hangings, beheadings, and dismemberments were less common than in 17th-century England, but they

certainly took place. The punishments that were meted out for serious crimes were very severe: burnings, brandings, and whippings. Pillorying (locking head and hands in a frame) was used for lesser crimes. A woman accused of "scolding" (nagging or quarreling noisily) was liable to be ducked in the village pond on a ducking-stool.

▲ Inmates at Connecticut's Newgate prison, named after a London prison, were expected to work long hours in the mines or workshops.

◀ The ducking-stool was another form of punishment imported from England. A woman who constantly nagged her husband could easily find herself tied to the ducking stool.

Colonial judges thought that wrong-doers should feel ashamed of their crime, and this influenced many of the punishments that were handed out. Burglars in Massachusetts, for example, were branded on the forehead with a hot iron in the shape of a "B." Married women who were unfaithful were sometimes forced to wear a scarlet letter "A"—for adulteress—on their clothes. Nathaniel Hawthorne's novel *The Scarlet Letter* is about a woman in colonial New England who is punished in this way for having an illegitimate child after an adulterous affair with a minister.

INJUSTICE

Some of the punishments faced by slaves who tried to escape were quite horrific. By the mid-18th century slaves outnumbered the white population in South Carolina, and the authorities greatly feared rebellion. In an attempt to prevent such an uprising in New York a law was passed in 1712 that prevented more than three slaves from congregating

◀ *Hester Prynne, the central character of Nathaniel Hawthorne's* The Scarlet Letter.

EYEWITNESS

DURING THE REVOLUTIONARY WAR LOYALTIES WERE STRONGLY DIVIDED. BRITISH SYMPATHIZERS OFTEN FOUND THEMSELVES ON TRIAL BY PATRIOTS.

" *The 6th of December at…New Jersey, Thomas Randolph, cooper, who had publickly proved himself an enemy to his country, by reviling and using his utmost endeavours to oppose the proceedings of Continental and Provincial Conventions and Committees, in defence of their rights and liberties; and he, being judged a person of not consequence enough for a severer punishment, was ordered to be stripped naked, well coated with tar and feathers, and carried in a wagon publickly round the town…as he soon became duly sensible of his offence for which he earnestly begged pardon…he was released. "*

together. A group of South Carolina slaves who mutinied in 1739 were blinded and mutilated. This was typical of the kind of justice colonial slaves could expect.

SEE ALSO

RELIGION, PURITAN ■ SALEM WITCH TRIALS ■ VIRGINIA COMPANY

HERNANDO DE SOTO

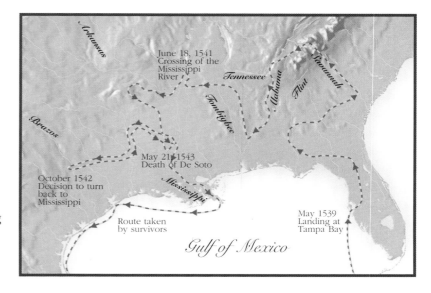

The Spanish *conquistador* (the Spanish word for conqueror) Hernando De Soto led the first European expedition to the banks of the Mississippi River and was also the first European to explore the southeastern part of the United States.

De Soto was born in the Spanish town of Badajoz in 1496. In 1514 he arrived at Panama and in the next two decades distinguished himself as a soldier and leader in the Spanish conquests of Nicaragua, Guatemala, the Yucatán, and Peru. De Soto returned to Spain in 1536 and was appointed governor of Cuba. In 1537 the king of Spain authorized him to conquer all the uncharted lands to the north of Cuba.

THE LONG MARCH BEGINS

De Soto left Spain on April 7, 1538, with 650 men and women. He arrived in Cuba in May and spent a year there before sailing to Tampa Bay on the west coast of Florida, where he landed in May 1539. From there his expedition began its long march northward. All along the route De Soto's soldiers were openly hostile toward the natives they encountered.

In the three years after his landing De Soto traveled 4,000 miles (6,400 km) across the southeastern part of the United States. Spurred on by native tales of a "land of gold," they marched from Florida to the Savannah River and followed its course into eastern Tennessee. Finding no gold, they turned south then back north again along the Tombigbee River. In the spring of 1541 De Soto crossed the Mississippi River and struggled through the swamplands of central Arkansas. The party spent the harsh winter of 1542 in a native Tula settlement near modern-day Camden, Arkansas, but by the following spring about half of De Soto's team had perished. The survivors crossed into Louisiana, near the confluence of the Red and Mississippi rivers, where De Soto contracted a serious fever. He died on May 21. His body was weighted down with sand and lowered into the Mississippi to hide it from local natives. De Soto's successor as leader of the expedition was a man named Luis de Moscoso. He led them west, and after sailing down the Mississippi in boats they had constructed, 311 survivors finally reached settlements in New Spain in September 1543.

SEE ALSO
FLORIDA ■ LOUISIANA ■ NEW SPAIN

▲ *After De Soto's arduous explorations of the 1540s, no more Europeans visited the Mississippi region for about a century.*

▼ *During De Soto's grueling march his party fought many battles with Native Americans. They also had to survive drought, harsh winter weather, illness, and disease.*

DECLARATION OF INDEPENDENCE

The Declaration of Independence, formally adopted by the Second Continental Congress on July 4, 1776, is the most famous document in American history. This "charter of freedom" has since provided the inspiration for independence movements throughout the world.

By the summer of 1776 the Revolutionary War with England had been raging for a year. The members of Congress were conducting the war from the Philadelphia State House (later to be renamed Independence Hall), from where they had to deal both with the war effort itself and with the problem of putting together long-term aims for the young American nation. Despite years of provocation by the British government, the

congressmen were naturally cautious about overturning the established system of government. If the British government had decided to make peace during the opening months of the war, it is possible that relations between the two countries could have been repaired. However, as the fighting continued through the early months of 1776, the British seemed determined to reassert their power over the colonies, and any such chance evaporated. As the months went by, Congress edged closer and closer to the final break.

On June 7, 1776, Richard Henry Lee of Virginia submitted a resolution to Congress declaring that "these United Colonies are, and of right ought to be, free and independent States, that they

▲ *The signing of the Declaration was the first momentous step on the path to an independent United States of America.*

are absolved of all allegiance to the British Crown" There was a delay in passing this resolution until July 2, but its outcome was never in doubt. On June 11 Congress appointed a committee of five to draft a statement in justification of Lee's resolution. The members of Congress were aware of the enormous step they were taking, and they wanted their reasons to be spelled out in the most persuasive manner possible. The five men appointed were Thomas Jefferson of Virginia, John Adams of Massachusetts, Benjamin Franklin of Pennsylvania, Robert Livingston of New York, and Roger Sherman of Connecticut.

DAWN OF A NEW ERA

On June 28 this committee reported back to Congress with the first draft of the document, written largely by Jefferson. After alterations had been made, the "Declaration of Independence," as it was named, was formally approved on July 4. The New York delegation could not initially take part in the vote, but on July 15 their representatives added their votes to make the resolution unanimous.

It is clear that the congressmen had a good case for independence. A large part of the document is a long list of specific grievances against King George and is a clear attempt by Jefferson to justify the decision to claim independence from the British. As he explained, "The history of the present King of Great Britain is a history of repeated injuries and usurpations, all having in direct object the establishment of an absolute tyranny over these states..." Not least among the charges is the fact that at the time the document was being written, King George was actively waging war against what were seen as his American subjects.

It is the first part of the document that is most often quoted. In it Jefferson expresses the moral foundation on which the Americans are making their case for independence. It is this preface to the

The Declaration Committee (from left to right): Thomas Jefferson, Roger Sherman, Ben Franklin, Robert Livingston, and John Adams.

Declaration of Independence that came to be recognized as one of the most inspired and eloquently expressed defenses of human rights.

A RESPECT OF NATURAL RIGHTS

The document starts by explaining a revolutionary view of the rights of individual people and the responsibilities and protection they could expect of their government. These were known as "natural rights." This view had lately become popular among 18th-century philosophers, and it stated that governments were morally obliged to respect the rights of people. If rulers failed to do this, they were no longer entitled to rule. It then explains that governments are set up for the purpose of securing these rights, and that if a government betrays the trust of the people, they should be allowed to get rid of it. In other words, people have the right to chose their own government. The Declaration of Independence was the first formal statement of this belief in history.

Although it was formally approved on July 4, the Declaration was not in fact signed until much later—it took several weeks for the members of Congress to add their signatures, and John Dickinson was the only one not to sign. In the final sentence of the Declaration the members pledged to each other "...our Lives, our Fortunes and our sacred Honor."

SEE ALSO
ADAMS, JOHN ■ AMERICAN REVOLUTIONARY WAR ■ CONTINENTAL CONGRESS ■ FRANKLIN, BENJAMIN ■ JEFFERSON, THOMAS

▶ *Aware of the momentous nature of the Declaration of Independence, Congress ordered the final draft to be inscribed on parchment.*

E Y E W I T N E S S

THE UNANIMOUS DECLARATION OF THE THIRTEEN UNITED STATES OF AMERICA

D

66 When, in the Course of human events, it becomes necessary for one people to dissolve the political bands which have connected them with another, and to assume, among the powers of the earth, the separate and equal station to which the Laws of Nature and of Nature's God entitle them, a decent respect to the opinions of mankind requires that they should declare the causes which impel them to the separation.

We hold these truths to be self-evident: That all men are created equal; that they are endowed by their Creator with certain unalienable Rights; that among these are Life, Liberty, and the pursuit of Happiness; that, to secure these rights, Governments are instituted among Men, deriving their just powers from the consent of the governed; That whenever any Form of Government becomes destructive of these ends, it is the Right of the People to alter or to abolish it, and to institute new Government, laying its foundation on such principles, and organizing its powers in such form, as to them shall seem most likely to effect their Safety and Happiness...99

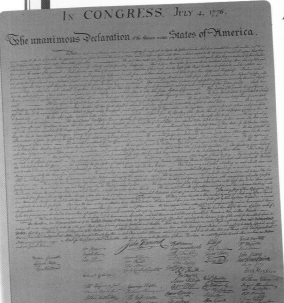

D DEERFIELD MASSACRE

Deerfield is in northwestern Massachusetts, on the Connecticut and Deerfield rivers. Settled in 1669 and incorporated as a town in 1673, it was one of the first towns in the upper Connecticut Valley and for much of the colonial period was the northwestern outpost of the New England frontier.

Deerfield's position made it particularly vulnerable to French and native raiders during Queen Anne's War (1702–1713), when England, the Netherlands, and Austria declared war on France and Spain. The French in America, supported by local natives, led many attacks in New England. In 1704 Deerfield was subject to a particularly devastating attack. A combined force burned the town, murdered 50 settlers, and took around a hundred more captive. During the grueling march to the native lands in Canada, many of the captives died. The remainder were held hostage and ransomed back to their community, although some did stay in Canada. The incident came to be known as the Deerfield Massacre.

A PURITAN SCANDAL

One noted survivor of the raid was the town's Puritan minister, John Williams, who wrote an account of his captivity entitled *The Redeemed Captive Returning to Zion*. The most famous survivor was his daughter Eunice, who grew up among her captors and, despite the efforts of her family, refused to be "redeemed." On her release she chose to remain with the tribe and married one of the

Mohawk tribesmen, bringing up their children as natives. Eunice Williams's case became a scandal throughout New England, especially since she was from a respected Puritan family.

SEE ALSO

MASSACHUSETTS ■ NEW ENGLAND ■ RELIGION, PURITAN ■ QUEEN ANNE'S WAR

▲ *The inhabitants of Deerfield were helpless against the ferocious attack carried out by Mohawks, Abenakis, and some French Canadians.*

DELAWARE

Delaware, situated on the Atlantic seaboard and the second smallest of the 13 colonies, played an important part in the early history of America. In spite of its size and troubled political history, Thomas Jefferson once called Delaware a "jewel among the states" in reference to the large areas of fertile agricultural land in the region.

Various Native-American tribes inhabited the area before Europeans arrived. The Munsee-speaking natives of the Delaware tribe lived in northern Delaware while the Nanticoke and Assateague filled the southern and coastal areas. As Europeans began to arrive in the region, these tribes withdrew to the west, and by the mid-18th century almost all of the native population had moved.

SWEDISH SETTLERS

In 1610 English ships sailed into Delaware Bay, although it was not until 1631 that Europeans attempted to settle in the region. The Dutch founded the settlement of Zwaanendael in 1631 but it was rapidly destroyed by native tribes.

In 1638 a group of Swedish settlers founded Fort Christina, the first permanent European settlement in Delaware, on the site now occupied by Wilmington. The settlement formed part of the territory known as New Sweden, which survived until it was captured by Dutch forces in 1655. The Delaware region then came under the control of the Dutch colony of New Netherland. A further upheaval came in 1664 during the Second Dutch War,

▲ *Delaware was named after Lord De La Warr, the first governor of Virginia.*

when English troops captured the colony of New Netherland and renamed it New York, bringing the region under English rule.

Eighteen years later, in 1682, the Duke of York granted the Delaware area to William Penn (the founder of Pennsylvania), allowing Pennsylvanian merchants greater access to the ports. At first, the union worked well, but as Pennsylvania's population grew, Delawareans became alarmed that they would be dominated by the parent colony. In order to calm these fears, Penn granted Delaware its own colonial assembly in 1704, although the two areas continued to have the same governor until 1776. The creation of the assembly made Delaware a separate colony, but despite their new independence, the population continued to be influenced

▲ *The Old Swede's Church in Wilmington, Delaware. It was built by Swedish settlers in 1698, although the cemetery had already been there for 60 years as a burial ground for the inhabitants of Fort Christina.*

by settlers in Pennsylvania, for example, by allowing religious groups to worship freely.

The two colonies also shared economic ties. The ports of northern Delaware assumed great importance during the colonial period since they formed a transportation link for the export of products from inland Pennsylvania to England. Settlers in southern Delaware were quick to exploit the rich agricultural lands. Slavery spread into the southern part of the colony as farmers formed relations with Maryland plantations. By the time of the American Revolution the colony was an important American shipping, agricultural, and industrial center.

During the Revolution many Delaware citizens served courageously in the Continental Army. One body of troops from Delaware earned the name "Blue Hen's Chickens" because their fighting spirit was compared to that of fighting Blue Hen's roosters.

▲ *A log cabin built in the early 18th century at Fort Christina, now known as Fort Christiana.*

However, not all Delawareans supported the revolutionary cause; many citizens remained loyal to Britain and worked against independence. As war raged across the land, Patriot farmers had to deal with hostile British troops and also Loyalist settlers attacking their farms and homesteads.

DELAWARE ACCEPTS A COMPROMISE

After the war Delaware heartily supported the idea of a Constitutional Convention. At the Convention John Dickinson and George Read of Delaware argued for equal representation in Congress for all states, regardless of their population. However, some delegates thought that the states should be represented according to the size of their population and their wealth. This scheme appealed to Massachusetts, Pennsylvania, and other large states, but it was fiercely resisted by small states such as Delaware and New Jersey, since they feared that it would give too much power to the larger states. After much debate a compromise was reached that Delaware accepted. On December 7, 1787, Delaware became the first of the states to ratify (approve) the new Constitution.

THE WIND OF CHANGE

In 1787 the Delaware state legislature passed a law that encouraged slaveholders to free their slaves. Slaveholders began to release large numbers of slaves, and by 1800 over half of Delaware's black population had been freed.

Various groups were behind the law: Quaker and Methodist religious groups helped convince state officials that slavery was against God's will. Added to these arguments were the ideals contained in the Declaration of Independence, which promoted liberty and equality for all—ideals that should extend to African Americans. There were also those who believed that banning slavery would be beneficial to the economy.

SEE ALSO
AMERICAN REVOLUTIONARY WAR
▨ CONSTITUTIONAL CONVENTION
▨ CONTINENTAL ARMY ▨ PENNSYLVANIA
▨ SLAVE TRADE

DETROIT

The French explorer Antoine de la Mothe Cadillac founded a settlement on the site of modern Detroit in 1701. He called it Fort Ponchartrain du détroit, or "Fort Ponchartrain of the strait," referring to its location on a strait of water (today known as the Detroit River) between Lakes Huron and Erie. Cadillac had high hopes for its future, even writing at one point that it would "become the Paris of New France."

Detroit became established as an important trading center for the fur trade. At the heart of this trade were French merchants who bought and exchanged goods for valuable otter, beaver, deer, fox, and muskrat skins trapped by natives. However, Detroit was slow to develop, and by the end of the French and Indian War it was still a relatively small settlement.

In 1763 the town was the target of an attack by the Ottawa tribe, but they failed in their attempt to capture it.

During the American Revolutionary War Detroit was the main base for Native Americans fighting as British agents against the American forces in western Pennsylvania and the Ohio Valley. The British governor Henry Hamilton was known as "the hair-buyer of Detroit" because of his willingness to pay for Patriot scalps. The fort remained in British control until the end of the war.

Under the terms of the Treaty of Paris of 1783 Detroit became part of the United States but remained in British hands. It was not until 1796, after Jay's Treaty agreed to withdraw all British forces from America, that a small American force arrived to take control of Detroit.

SEE ALSO
AMERICAN REVOLUTIONARY WAR
■ COUREURS DE BOIS ■ FRENCH AND
INDIAN WAR ■ FUR TRADE ■ JAY, JOHN
■ TREATY OF PARIS 1783

▼ *Antoine de la Mothe Cadillac landing at the site of present-day Detroit, where Cobo Hall now stands.*

FURTHER READING

Anderson, Joan. **A Williamsburg Household**. *New York: Clarion Books, 1988.*

Barrett, Tracy. **Growing up in Colonial America**. *Brookfield, Connecticut: The Milbrook Press, 1995.*

Bosco, Peter L. **Roanoke: The Lost Colony**. *Brookfield, Connecticut: The Milbrook Press, 1992.*

Bowen, Gary. **Stranded at Plimoth Plantation 1629**. *New York: HarperCollins Publishers, 1994.*

Carter, Alden R. **The Colonial Wars**. *New York: Franklin Watts, 1992.*

Clare, John D., ed. **The Voyages of Christopher Columbus**. *San Diego: Gulliver Books (HBJ), 1992.*

Daugherty, James. **The Landing of the Pilgrims**. *New York: Random House, 1978.*

Erdosh, George. **Food & Recipes of the 13 Colonies**. *New York: PowerKids Press, 1997.*

Fritz, Jean. **The Double Life of Pocahontas**. *New York: Puffin Books, 1983.*

Hakim, Joy. **The First Americans**. *New York: Oxford University Press, 1993.*

Hakim, Joy. **Making Thirteen Colonies**. *New York: Oxford University Press, 1993.*

Hakim, Joy. **From Colonies to Country**. *New York: Oxford University Press, 1993.*

Kalman, Bobbie. **Colonial Life**. *New York: Crabtree Publishing, 1992.*

Kalman, Bobbie. **Historic Communities: A Colonial Town—Williamsburg**. *New York: Crabtree Publishing, 1992.*

Kent, Deborah. **African Americans in the Thirteen Colonies**. *New York: Childrens Press, 1988.*

Lenski, Lois. **Indian Captive: The Story of Mary Jemison**. *New York: HarperTrophy, 1969.*

Roach, Marilynne K. **In the Days of the Salem Witchcraft Trials**. *Boston: Houghton Mifflin Co., 1996.*

Roop, Connie and Peter, eds. **Pilgrim Voices: Our First Year in the New World**. *New York: Walkers and Company, 1995.*

Tunis, Edwin. **Shaw's Fortune: The Picture Story of a Colonial Plantation**. *Cleveland: The World Publishing Company, 1966.*

Speare, Elizabeth George. **The Witch of Blackbird Pond**. *Boston: Houghton Mifflin Co., 1958.*

Washburne, Carolyn Kott. **A Multicultural Portrait of Colonial Life**. *New York: Marshall Cavendish, 1994.*

Waters, Kate. **Tapenum's Day: A Wampanoag Indian Boy in Pilgrim Times**. *New York: Scholastic Press, 1996.*

Yenne, Bill, ed. **Our Colonial Period: The Chronicle of American History from 1607 to 1770**. *San Francisco: Bluewood Books, 1996.*

SET INDEX

Volume numbers and main entries are shown in **bold**. Page numbers of illustrations or captions are shown in *italic* or ***bold italic*** if they are in main articles.

A

Abercrombie, General **3**:213–15
Acadia 1:*4–5*, **6**:437, **7**:535
  see also Port Royal
Acoma **7**:497, **7**:498, **8**:601
Adams, Abigail **9**:*681*
Adams, John 1:*6*, **1**:42, **1**:62, **2**:*146*, **9**:704
Adams, Samuel 1:*7*, **1**:62, **1**:64, **2**:*117*, **5**:366, **9**:703
Africa **9**:*683*, **9**:691–92
African Americans *see* black population; free blacks; slave culture; slave trade; slavery
Aix-la-Chapelle, Peace of **5**:345, **7**:534
Alaska 1:*8–9*, **1**: 51, **8**:*630*
Albany Congress 1:10, **5**:339
alcohol **3**:*199*, **3**:200, **4**:246, **5**:388, **9**:689
Aleuts **1**:8-9, **5**:327, **10**:778
Alexander, William **1**:4, **7**:*533*
alfalfa **3**:202
Algonquians 1:*11–16*, **2**:118, **5**:346, **5**:361, **7**:510, **9**:644
Allen, Ethan 1:*17*, **1**:19, **7**:491, **10**:755-56
Allouez, Claude Jean **9**:648
almanacs **1**:*53*, **1**:55, **6**:422, **6**:425, **7**:523–24
Altham, John **6**:451
Alvarado, Hernando de **7**:497

Amadas, Philip **7**:526
American Fur Company **3**:*224*
American Revolutionary War 1:*18–28*, **5**:*388*
  and Anglicanism **8**:611
  British sympathizers **2**:143
  and the Cherokee **2**:98-9, **5**:343
  and the Iroquois **1**:67, **5**:333, **5**:382
  and King George III **4**:244
  minutemen **6**:*445*
  money **6**:455
  and Quakers **8**:629
  and the theater **8**:577
  see also Continental Army; Loyalists; Paris, Treaty of (1783)
Amherst, Jeffrey **3**:214, **6**:460–61, **7**:*514*
Amish **4**:*288*, **7**:548, **8**:617
Andros, Edmund **1**:59, **2**:*118*, **2**:120, **3**:*167*
Anglicans 2:*108*, **8**:*610–11*, **10**:761
  and the Chesapeake **4**:277-8, church-state relations **2**:107–9
  and marriages **6**:405–7
Annapolis Convention 1:*29*
Anne, Queen *see* Queen Anne's War
Anticosti **5**:340

Apache 1:*30–31*, **7**:498–99
apothecaries **6**:*423*
Appalachian Mts. **3**:*217*, **3**:*218*
apprenticeships 1:*32–33*, **1**:*55*, **2**:103–5, **5**:385, **6**:425–26
architecture 1:*34–39*, **1**:*54*, **4**:*285*, **4**:289
Argall, Samuel **2**:90
Arizona, **8**:*597*
  see also Pueblo
Arnold, Benedict 1:17, **1**:19–20, **1**:*40*, **2**:126, **9**:*663*, **9**:664
Arteaga, Ignacio **1**:51
Articles of Confederation 1:29, **1**:*41–43*, **2**:122, **2**:129
artisans **9**:*700*, **9**:702
artists *see* painting
asiento **9**:690
assemblies, law **4**:251–52
Assiniboine **6**:*426*
Astor, John Jacob **3**:224
astronomy **9**:*673*
Athapaskan tribe **1**:8
Attucks, Crispus **3**:*211*
audiencias **7**:506
Augustus Adolphus **7**:509
Aumont, Simon François d' **7**:487
Avilés, Pedro Menéndez de **3**:196, **6**:446, **7**:*507*, **9**:656

B

backcountry/backwoods **3**:217
Bacon's Rebellion 1:*44–45*, **4**:280, **10**:*761*
Balbao, Nunez de **10**:772–73
Baltimore 1:*46–47*, **6**:444
Baltimore Road **9**:654
banks **6**:455
Baptists 2:*107*, **4**:259, **8**:*612–13*, **9**:645
Barbados, slavery **9**:693-4
Barlowe, Arthur **7**:526
bartering **6**:443, **6**:452–53
Bartgis, Matthias **7**:524
Bartram, John and William **8**:566, **9**:*671–72*
baseball **3**:231
Beaujeau, Daniel de **9**:*679*
Beissel, Johann Conrad **6**:463
Belcher, Jonathan **7**:495
Bemis Heights, Battle of **2**:*127*, **9**:664
Bennington, Battle of **10**:756
Bering, Vitus Jonassen 1:8–9, **1**:*48–49*
Bering Strait **1**:48
Berkeley, William **1**:44, **1**:*45*, **10**:*761*
Bible **1**:15, **6**:450, **6**:*451*, **8**:617
Bienville, Jean-Baptiste le Moyne, Sieur de 1:*50*, **5**:379, **7**:504

Bill of Rights (1689) **4**:248
Bill of Rights (1791) **2**:109, **4**:265
Billings, William **6**:464
Biloxi tribe **5**:379
Bimini **8**:582
black population 8:*584–86*, **9**:*682*, **10**:730
see also free blacks; slavery
"Blackbeard" see Teach, Edward
Blainville, Pierre Joseph de **3**:213
Blair, James **9**:669, **10**:781
Blaxton, William **1**:60
Block, Adriaen **2**:118, **9**:644, **9**:*645*
Bloody Marsh, Battle of **7**:536
boats *see* river travel
Bodega y Quadra, Juan Francisco de la 1:9, **1**:*51*
Bonaparte, Napoleon **5**:380
books *see* libraries and books
Boone, Daniel 1:*56–57*, **3**:*223*, **5**:*342*
Boscawen, Edward **5**:376
Boston 1:*58–61*, **6**:418, **9**:*704*
bank **6**:455
black population **8**:585
book trade **1**:54
churches **8**:*610*
furniture **2**:136
Irish immigrants **4**:*293*
port **6**:*416*, **6**:418
post office **8**:*593–94*
silverware **2**:138
Boston Massacre 1:6, **1**:7, **1**:*62*, **3**:*211*, **6**:418
Boston Port Act 1:7, **1**:61, **1**:64, **5**:325
Boston Post Road **8**:*593*
Boston Tea Party 1:7, **1**:61, **1**:*63–64*, **2**:128, **6**:*416*
Bouquet, Colonel **1**:*16*
Bowdoin, James **9**:*681*
Bowne, John **7**:*516*
Braddock, Edward **3**:213–14, **3**:*221*, **9**:678, **9**:*679*
Bradford, William 1:*65*, **3**:189, **5**:*357*, **5**:369, **6**:415, **8**:579–80, **10**:737
Bradstreet, Anne 1:66
Brandywine Creek, Battle of **1**:22–24, **2**:126–27, **2**:130
Brant, Chief Joseph **1**:*67*
Brant, Molly **5**:*339*
Bray, Thomas **1**:54
Brebeuf, Jean de **6**:*447–50*
Brethren, Church of the **8**:617
Bridges, Charles **7**:*543*
British East India Company **1**:64
Brown, James **6**:432, **6**:*433*
bubonic plague **3**:164
buccaneers *see* piracy
buckskins **3**:*222-23*
buffalo **1**:15, **4**:270
Bulfinch, Charles **1**:*58*
Bunker Hill, Battle of 1:19, **1**:*68–69*
Burgesses *see* House of Burgesses
Burgoyne, John 1:22–23,

1:*70*, **2**:127, **9**:*663*, **9**:664
Burke, Edmund **5**:*325*
Burr, Aaron **4**:*261*
Burroughs, George **9**:658
Bushell, John **7**:535
Butler, John **5**:*382*
Byllinge, Edward **7**:492
Byrd, Evelyn **9**:*702*
Byrd, William **9**:700
Byrd II, William 1:38, **1**:*52–53*, **1**:*71*, **9**:700, **10**:*757*

C

cabildos **4**:257
cabinetmakers **2**:136, **3**:226-27
Cabot, John 1:4, **2**:*84*, **4**:306, **7**:*520*
Cabrillo, Joao Rodrigues **2**:85
Caddo Confederacy **10**:734-35
cajuns **1**:5, **4**:*284*, **8**:592
Calusa **3**:196
Calvert, Cecil **6**:*408*
Calvert, George **1**:46, **4**:252, **5**:357, **6**:408-09
Calvert, Leonard **6**:408, **6**:409
Calvin, John **4**:298
Campbell, John **7**:522
canoes **1**:12, **1**:*14*, **9**:*648-50*
Cape Breton Island **1**:4, **2**:88, **3**:214, **7**:533, **7**:*535*
Carleton, Guy **5**:*383*, **6**:461
Carrier, Sarah **9**:660
Carroll, Charles, III **1**:47, **4**:*293*, **8**:*615*
Carroll, Daniel **8**:615
Carter, John **9**:700
Carter, "King" **9**:700, **10**:*759*
Carteret, George **7**:*492*, **7**:493
Cartier, Jacques 2:*88–89*, **4**:*273*, **4**:281, **6**:458-59, **7**:*484*, **7**:*485*
and Quebec City **8**:604
Carver, John **1**:14, **1**:65, **6**:421, **8**:*579*
Catawbas **3**:171
Catholics 2:108, **2**:109, **6**:408-9, **6**:410, **8**:*614–15*
see also Franciscans; Jesuits; missionaries
cattle **3**:186, **5**:*370*
Champlain, Samuel de 1:4, **2**:*90–91*, **4**:281, **10**:*755*
and Annapolis Royal **7**:*484-85*
mapping by **1**:58, **2**:90, **10**:*771*
and Montreal and Quebec **2**:91, **6**:458, **7**:*485*, **8**:604-5
Charles I **4**:*306*, **6**:408, **8**:593
Charles II **1**:45, **2**:120
and Carolina **7**:527, **9**:705
and the Hudson's Bay Company **4**:*268*
and Massachusetts **6**:417
and New Netherland **7**:503
and Pennsylvania **5**:356-57, **7**:*546-47*
Charles Stuart, Prince **4**:*297*
Charleston 2:*92–94*, **9**:*707*

Battle of **2**:93, **9**:*705*, **9**:707
harbor **6**:*430*
merchants **6**:432,
rice exports from **9**:649
Scots-Irish immigrants **4**:*300*
siege of (1780) **2**:93, **5**:352,
slaves **9**:*690*
Charlestown **7**:*490*
Charter Oak **2**:120
Charter of Privileges **7**:547
Chase, Samuel **1**:47
Chatte, Aymar de **2**:90
Cherokee 2:*95–99*, **3**:*219*, **5**:342-43
and Daniel Boone **1**:56–57
and diseases **2**:96, **3**:171, **4**:245
medicine **6**:426
religion **8**:620
Chesapeake Bay area **4**:275–80, **6**:*411*
boats **9**:650
fishing **3**:193–94
slave labour **9**:693, **9**:695–96
see also Maryland; Virginia
Chickasaw **5**:342
chickens **5**:371
children 2:100–105
games **3**:228–29
and the Salem Witch Trials **9**:659–60
sent to the colonies **4**:310
slave **2**:100, **8**:585, **9**:669, **10**:*727*
see also apprenticeships; family life; schools and colleges
Chirikov, Alexei **1**:8–9, **1**:48–49
Choctaw **3**:230, **5**:379
Chomedey de Maisonneuve, Paul de **6**:458, **6**:459, **6**:*460*
Chrikov, Alexei **1**:48–49
Christmas **3**:189, **3**:191, **3**:230
Church of the Brethren **8**:617
Church of Scotland **4**:298
church-state relations 2:*106–9*, **4**:278
churches and missions **1**:35–36, **4**:*280*, **6**:446–47, **8**:*598*, **8**:*614*, **10**:*735*
Anglican **8**:*610*
Californian **2**:86-7, **7**:*508*, **8**:*630*
and education **9**:668–69
and land **5**:*357*, **5**:358–59
Presbyterian **8**:624, **8**:*625*
Cibola **2**:131, **8**:*600*, **10**:734–35
Clark, Ann **6**:407
class *see* social structure
Clinton, Henry **1**:24, **1**:25, **2**:130, **6**:456, **9**:664
and Benedict Arnold **1**:40
cloth **2**:134, **5**:*389*, **5**:*390*, **6**:*466*
clothing 2:110–13, **5**:386
children's **2**:*101*, **2**:103
Moravian **8**:616
Native-American **1**:12, **5**:*330-1*,
Quaker **8**:628
uniforms **1**:*26*, **6**:*440*
cock-fighting **3**:228, **3**:*231*

coffee houses **7**:*521*
coins **6**:417, **6**:452-55
Colbert, Jean-Baptiste 2:*114*, **7**:486–87
Colden, Cadwallader **1**:55, **7**:*515*
colleges *see* schools and colleges
Columbus, Christopher 2:*115–16*, **5**:371, **7**:*532*, **10**:726, **10**:738, **10**:*771–72*
Comanche **10**:735
Committee of Thirteen **1**:41
Committees of Correspondence 2:*117*
Company of New France **4**:254, **6**:488, **7**:485–86
Company of the West **5**:378–79, **7**:504
Concord *see* Lexington and Concord, Battles of
Congregational Church **8**:624
see also Puritans
Connecticut 2:*118–21*, **6**:416-17
black population **3**:210–11
commodity money **6**:453
government **4**:249, **4**:253
land allocation **5**:358
slavery **9**:693–94
conquistadores **4**:302, **6**:435
constitution
Federal (1787) **2**:*123*, **2**:129, **5**:373, **9**:647, **9**:681
first *see* Articles of Confederation
Constitutional Convention 2:*122–23*, **2**:129, **2**:150, **9**:681
Continental Army 1:18–19, **1**:41, **2**:*124–27*, **2**:150
and the Articles of Confederation **1**:*42*
and the militia **6**:440
training **10**:754
uniforms **1**:*26*
see also American Revolutionary War
Continental Congress 1:55, **2**:*128–29*
First **2**:128-29
Second **1**:41, **2**:128–29, **8**:594
and slavery **9**:696
Cook, James **1**:9, **4**:*264*, **7**:532
Copley, John Singleton **7**:*542-4*
Corey, Giles **9**:659
corn **3**:183, **3**:*184*, **3**:187, **3**:198, **3**:201
and Native Americans **5**:330
Cornbury, Lord **2**:107, **8**:610
Cornwallis, Charles 1:25, **1**:26–27, **2**:*130*, **7**:529, **10**:751, **10**:*789–90*
Coronada, Francisco Vasquez de 2:*131*, **7**:496–98, **8**:*600*
Corte Real, Miguel **9**:644
Cortes, Hernando **4**:302-3, **7**:506
mistress and son **6**:*435*
Cosby, William **10**:791
cotton **4**:*310*, **8**:585, **9**:646
Cotton, John **2**:107

Country Quakers **8**:565
***coureurs de bois* 2**:*132–33*,
  3:218, **3**:223
courts **2**:140, **2**:141–42, **4**:256
Cowpens, Battle of **9**:*708*
crafts 2:*134–39*, **5**:385–86
  see also apprenticeships;
    manufacturing; painting
Creek **3**:196, **4**:*247*
creoles **6**:436
**crime and punishment
  2**:*140–43*
  courts **2**:140, **2**:141–42, **4**:256
  criminals sent to the colonies
    4:310, **6**:412
  see also Salem Witch Trials
Cromwell, Oliver **4**:*290*, **6**:410,
  8:618
crops *see* corn; cotton; farming;
  indigo; plantations; rice;
  tobacco
Crozat, Antoine **5**:378
Cumberland Gap **1**:56-7, **3**:*218*
Cumberland House **4**:*268-69*
Cuming, Alexander **2**:96–97
currency *see* money

D
Dale, Thomas **8**:581
dancing **3**:230, **8**:*586*
Dare, Eleanor **9**:655
Dare, Virginia **7**:*526-7*, **9**:655
Dartmouth College **7**:*491*
Dawes, William **5**:366, **8**:631
De La Warr, Thomas West
  2:*149*, **4**:*253*, **5**:334–35
de Soto, Hernando 2:*144*,
  5:377, **5**:391
Deane, Silas **3**:209
**Declaration of
  Independence 2**:128-9,
  2:*145–47*, **4**:262, **5**:337–38,
  5:368
  and slavery **2**:150
Deerfield Massacre 2:*148*
Deganawidato **5**:328
Delaware 2:*149–50*,
  4:299–300, **7**:*546*, **8**:*585*,
  8:590–91
Delaware tribe **7**:548, **7**:549
Detroit 2:*151*, **3**:*214*
Dickinson, John **1**:42, **1**:*43*,
  2:147, **2**:150
Dinwiddie, Robert **3**:213, **4**:296
disease 1:60, **3**:*164–66*, **6**:422
  and Native Americans **3**:164,
    3:*165*, **3**:*166*, **3**:171, **4**:273,
    7:507, **8**:588–89
  see also medicine; smallpox
divorce **6**:406-7
doctors **6**:425–26, **9**:*674*, **9**:701
**Dominion of New England
  3**:*167*, **7**:513
Douglass, David **8**:575
Dragging-Canoe **5**:343
Drake, Francis 2:85–86,
  3:*168*, **3**:*197*, **8**:569, **9**:656,
  10:738
Drucour, Augustin Boschenry
  de **5**:376
Du Chambon, Louis **5**:345

du Sable, Jean Baptiste **9**:683
du Troyes, Chevalier **5**:351
Dudley, Joseph **3**:167, **8**:608
Dunkers **8**:617
Dunlap, William **8**:575, **8**:576
Dunmore, Lord **3**:219, **10**:781
Dutch East India Company
  7:500
Dutch Reformed Church **4**:258
Dutch West India Company
  7:500, **7**:502, **7**:503, **7**:510,
  8:618, **10**:*742*

E
Earl, Ralph **7**:544
East Indies **2**:115–16
education *see* schools and
  colleges
Edwards, Jonathan 3:*169*,
  4:258
Egginton, Elizabeth **7**:540
El Dorado **8**:609
Election Day **3**:189, **10**:766–67
Eliot, John **1**:15, **5**:347, **5**:348,
  6:450–51, **8**:*627*
Elizabeth I **3**:168, **3**:228, **4**:298,
  8:609
encomienda **7**:499
Endicott, John **1**:58, **4**:*249*
English (language) **5**:361–63
**English immigration
  4**:*275–80*, **4**:306-7, **8**:590
  advertised **4**:275, **4**:287–88,
    6:*409*
  and courts **2**:141–42
  and land **4**:279–80, **5**:355–58
  and social class **9**:700
  see also Chesapeake Bay
    area; New England;
    Plymouth Colony and the
    Pilgrims
enumerated goods **6**:470–71,
  9:649, **9**:699
environment 3:*170–75*
Episcopal Church **8**:611
Equiano, Olaudah 3:*176–77*
Eriksson, Leif **6**:414
Eskimo (Inuit) 1:8, **5**:*326–27*
Estevanico **7**:496, **9**:682,
  10:*734*
Eutaw Springs, Battle of **4**:260

F
Fairfax County Resolves **6**:413,
  10:769
Fallen Timbers, Battle of **7**:*530*,
  7:531, **9**:679
family life 1:52, **3**:*178–81*,
  6:423–24, **6**:464
  Native American **3**:181,
    8:588, **8**:*589*
  slave **3**:181, **9**:*682*, **9**:684–85
  see also children; marriage;
    women's roles
farming 3:170, **3**:171–74,
  3:*182–87*, **3**:198
  conflict with trappers **3**:224
  "exempt farms" **4**:291
  farmers in society **9**:701–2
  Native-American **4**:272,
    5:329–30, **5**:*355*, **6**:466–67

seigneurial system **6**:460,
  9:702
tenant farmers **5**:357
and women **3**:186, **4**:*308*
see also crops; land;
  livestock; milling
Fauquier, Francis **4**:*254*
Feke, Robert **7**:*541*, **7**:542
Fenwick, John **7**:492
festivals 3:*188–91*, **3**:200
  see also Thanksgiving
Few, James **7**:529
fishing 3:*192–95*, **3**:229,
  3:231, **6**:417–18
  by Native Americans **3**:170,
    3:*193*
  in Newfoundland **3**:175,
    3:192, **7**:520
Fitzhugh, William **6**:429
FitzSimons, Thomas **8**:615
flax **2**:136, **4**:*310*, **5**:390
Fleet, Thomas **6**:465
Florida 3:*196–97*, **6**:446–47
  Native Americans **3**:196,
    6:*404*, **6**:447, **6**:*452*, **8**:*582*,
    8:*621*
  see also St. Augustine
food and drink 2:*135*,
  3:*198–202*, **3**:231
forestry 3:*170*, **3**:172, **3**:*173*,
  3:*203–5*, **6**:469
forgers **2**:140
Fort Caroline **3**:196, **9**:656
Fort Christina **4**:*307*
Fort Duquesne **3**:213–14
Fort Frontenac **5**:353
Fort King George **4**:246
Fort Louisbourg *see* Louisbourg
Fort Michilimackinac **3**:218
Fort Necessity, Battles of **3**:213
Fort Oswego **3**:214
Fort Santa Elena **9**:705
Fort Ticonderoga, Battles of
  (1758) **3**:213–15, **6**:*457*
  (1759) **7**:*514*, **7**:*515*
  (1775) **1**:*17*, **1**:19, **10**:756
  (1777) **1**:22
Fort William Henry, Battle of
  3:214, **6**:457
forts, Spanish **5**:358, **5**:*359*
Fountain of Youth **8**:582
Fox, George **8**:628
France **1**:23, **1**:25–27, **4**:*303*,
  4:304–6
Francis I **2**:88, **2**:89, **4**:281
Franciscans **2**:86–87, **6**:446,
  6:447, **7**:485, **8**:614, **9**:661
Serra, Father Junipero 9:*675*
Franklin, Benjamin 1:6,
  2:*122*, **2**:146, **3**:*207–9*
  almanac **1**:*53*, **3**:208,
    7:523–24
  apprenticeship **1**:33, **1**:*55*,
    3:207
  and colonial union **1**:*10*
  and freedom of the press
    7:522–23
  libraries and books **1**:*53*,
    1:*54-55*, **3**:208
  and merchants **6**:433
  and music **6**:464

and Pennsylvania **7**:549,
  7:550, **8**:566
and the postal service **8**:594
the scientist **9**:672–73, **9**:*674*
Franklin, James **7**:523
free blacks 3:*210–11*
Freeman's Farm, Battle of **1**:70,
  9:664
Frelinghuysen, Theodorus
  4:258
French colonies *see* New
  France
**French immigration
  4**:*281–84*, **4**:*303*, **7**:485-7
  see also Acadia; Louisiana;
    New France
**French and Indian War
  3**:*212–15*, **4**:284, **4**:307,
  7:*489*, **10**:748
  and the Cherokee **2**:98
  ending *see* Paris, Treaty of
    (1763)
  and Georgia **4**:246
  and the Iroquois **1**:10, **1**:16,
    3:212–13, **5**:333
  metis expelled from Acadia
    6:437
  and the Shawnee **9**:678–79
French Revolution **7**:539
Frobisher, Martin **5**:*326*, **7**:*532*
**Frontenac, Comte Louis de
  3**:*216*, **5**:350–53, **7**:487–88
frontier 2:*113*, **3**:*217–19*
  immigrants at **4**:288, **4**:291
  marriages at **6**:405–6
  see also Northwest Ordinance
funerals 3:189, **3**:*220–21*
fur trade 3:*222–24*,
  10:*742-43*, **10**:*745*
  and canoes **9**:650
  and King Philip's War **5**:347-8
  and La Salle **5**:353
  and Louis de Frontenac **3**:216
  and Native Americans
    1:15–16, **2**:*133*, **3**:*223*,
    4:273, **4**:282, **6**:*431*, **8**:587,
    10:*744*
  in New France **2**:*132–33*,
    3:218, **3**:223, **4**:282, **4**:283
  St. Lawrence River **2**:90
  and wildlife **3**:174–75
  see also Boone, Daniel;
    Hudson's Bay Company
furniture 2:136–37, **3**:*225–27*

G
Gage, Thomas **1**:61, **1**:64, **1**:68,
  1:69, **5**:366
game, hunting **4**:271
games and sports 3:*228–31*
  Native-American **2**:98, **3**:188,
Gates, Horatio **1**:22, **4**:260,
  9:*663*, **9**:664
Gates, Thomas **2**:140
Gazley, Martha **2**:135
George II **4**:*295*, **5**:*344*
George III 1:*22*, **2**:*129*, **4**:*244*,
  7:*525*, **9**:*709*
George IV **4**:244
Georgia 4:*245–47*, **7**:536
  Anglicanism **2**:107

government 4:249, 4:252-4
Loyalists 5:382
merchants 6:432
plantations 4:247, 9:649
settlers 3:219, 4:245, 4:287,
   4:297, 8:619
slaves 4:311, 9:683
see also Oglethorpe, James
**German immigration 4:285
–89**
German Reformed Church
  8:616
**German sects 4:285–86, 6:404,
6:451, 7:548, 8:616–17**
German settlers 2:137, 3:187,
  3:204, 9:667
Germantown, Battle of
  2:126–27, 5:383
Gilbert, Humphrey 7:520,
  8:609
Gilliat, Sy 6:465
Gladwin, Major 8:583
glass 2:138–39, 5:387
Glassford, John 10:740
**Glorious Revolution (1688)
4:248, 4:299, 6:419**
  and Leisler's Rebellion 5:365
  repeated in Maryland 6:410
Goddard, William 8:594
Good, Sarah 9:658
Gosnold, Bartholomew 6:414
**government, colonial
4:249–54**
  French 2:114, 4:254, 7:486
  Spanish 4:254, 7:506–7
**government, local 4:255–57,
4:279**
  see also voting
Grant, James 10:751
grapes 3:185, 3:200
Grasse, Admiral de 1:27
**Great Awakening 2:109,
4:258–59, 6:451, 10:779**
  and the Baptists 8:612–13
  and the Presbyterians 8:624
  and the Puritans 8:627
  see also Edwards, Jonathan;
    Whitefield, George
Great Britain 4:278, 9:652
  American Revolution 1:26
  imperial policy 4:306–7, 7:525
  smuggling to 9:699
  see also Glorious Revolution
Great Compromise 2:122–23
Great Eastern Road 9:654
Great Northern Expedition 1:48
Great Philadelphia Wagon
  Road 8:566
Great Swamp Fight 5:348,
  5:349, 9:645
Great Valley 3:218-19, 4:301
Green Mountain Boys 1:17,
  1:22, 7:491, 10:755–56
**Greene, Nathanael 1:25,
2:130, 4:260, 5:374, 7:529,
9:708**
Greenland, Inuit 5:326, 5:327
Greenville, Treaty of 7:531
Grenville, George 8:596, 9:709
Grenville, Richard 7:526–27,
  9:655

Groseilliers, Médard de 4:268
Guilford Courthouse, Battle of
  4:301, 7:529
guilds 1:33, 5:385
gunsmiths 2:137, 5:388
Guy Fawkes Day 3:190
Guzman, Nuno de 7:506

H
Hakluyt, Richard 10:738
Halifax, Nova Scotia 7:534–35
Hallam family (actors) 8:576–77
**Hamilton, Alexander 4:261,
6:455**
Hamilton, Andrew 7:523,
  7:548, 10:791
Hamilton, Henry 2:151
**Hancock, John 1:64, 4:262,
5:366**
Hancock, Thomas 6:433
Handel, George Frederick
  6:464
Harris, Benjamin 7:522, 9:666
Harrower, John 4:311
Hart, Nancy 10:785
Hartford Colony 2:119
Harvard, John 1:53, 4:263
**Harvard College 1:53, 4:263,
9:668, 9:669, 9:671**
harvest festivals 10:736
Hat Act 5:389–90
Hawaii 4:264
Hawthorne, Nathaniel 2:143
headright system 5:355–357
health 6:423–24
  see also disease; medicine
hemp 5:390
Henrietta Maria (consort of
  England) 6:408
Henry IV (King of France)
  2:90
Henry VII 4:306
Henry VIII 3:228
**Henry, Patrick 2:117, 4:265,
5:337, 10:731, 10:760**
Herrod, James 5:343
Hesselius, Gustavus 7:543
Hessians 4:266, 5:374
  Battle of Trenton 1:21–22,
   10:751, 10:752
Hiawatha 5:331
Hispaniola 3:164, 10:771,
  10:772, 10:776
Hodgkinson, John 8:576
Holburne, Francis 5:376
Holmes, Obadiah 2:107
Hooker, Thomas 2:119
Hopi 6:468, 8:601-02, 8:621
Hopkins, Esek 9:647
Hopkins, Stephen 9:647
horses 4:270, 5:370, 5:371,
  9:646, 10:735
hospitals 6:427
House of Burgesses 4:253,
  4:278–79, 10:758, 10:764–65
  and Patrick Henry 4:265
Houston, Sam 4:301
Howe, Richard 1:21, 5:374
Howe, William 1:19, 1:20–21,
  1:24, 1:68, 9:663, 10:750–51
Hudson, Henry 4:267, 7:492,

7:500, 7:510, 7:532
Hudson River 5:360
**Hudson's Bay Company
3:222, 4:268–69, 4:283,
5:390**
  and the Inuit 5:327
  and mixed-race marriages
   6:437
  and Native Americans 1:15-16
  see also fur trade
Huguenots 4:284, 9:706
Hull, John 9:701
Hundred Associates see
  Company of New France
Hunter, Richard 8:575
hunting 2:113, 4:270–71
  see also food and drink; fur
   trade
Huron 4:272–73
  alliance with the French 2:90,
   2:91, 4:273, 4:282
  and Catholicism 6:449, 6:450
  and diseases 4:273, 6:449
  and Jacques Cartier 4:273,
   6:458
  and Montreal 6:458
  rivals of the Iroquois 4:273,
   4:282, 5:333
**Hutchinson, Anne 2:119,
4:274, 4:280, 9:645**
Hutchinson, Thomas 1:64,
  2:117, 9:704
Hyde, Edward 7:526

I
Iberville, Pierre le Moyne, Sieur
  d' 3:191, 5:351, 5:378
Ile Royale see Cape Breton
  Island
Illinois 4:284, 7:531
Illinois tribe 1:15, 5:379, 5:391
Impartial Administration of
  Justice, Act for the 5:325
imperial policy 4:302–7
  English 4:306–7, 7:525
  French 4:303–6, 7:486
  Spanish 4:302–4, 7:506–7
**indentured servants 3:210,
4:275–76, 4:308–11,
5:356–57, 9:692–93, 10:758**
  black 8:584
  children as 9:668–69
  Irish 4:291, 4:292–93
  replaced by slaves 4:311,
   5:693
  in society 9:702
Indians see Native Americans
**indigo 4:247, 5:324, 8:572,
9:695, 9:707**
Ingoldsby, Richard 5:365
innoculations 6:419
inns and taverns 3:199, 3:231
**Intolerable Acts (1774) 1:64,
2:128, 4:247, 5:325, 7:525**
Inuit (Eskimo) 1:8, 5:326–27
**Irish immigration 4:290–93,
8:615**
iron 5:387–88
Iron Act (1750) 5:388
**Iroquois Confederacy 3:216,
5:328–33, 6:450, 6:460, 7:486**

J
Jacobite Rebellion 4:295–97
Jacobs, George 9:659
Jamaica 5:383, 9:694
James I 1:4, 3:190, 4:298–99,
  4:305, 8:609
James II 3:167, 4:248, 4:299,
  8:607
James, Thomas 9:703–4
**Jamestown 5:334–35, 10:743,
10:759–60**
  first settlers 4:275, 4:276,
   5:344, 8:589, 10:758-60
  and John Smith 9:697
  legislative assembly 4:250
  slaves/indentured servants
   9:689, 9:691, 10:758-59
  and tobacco 10:738–39,
   10:744
Jay, John 5:336
Jay's Treaty (1794) 2:151,
  5:336
**Jefferson, Thomas 1:6, 2:117,
2:146–47, 5:337–38**
  book collection 1:53
  education 9:667–68
  and religious freedom 2:109
  and Shays's Rebellion 9:681
  and Tadeusz Kosciuszko
   5:352
Jesuits 4:282, 6:446, 6:448,
  6:449–51, 7:507, 8:615
  see also Marquette, Jacques;
   missionaries
**Jewish religion 8:618–19,
9:645**
**Johnson, William 5:333,
5:339, 5:345**
Johnston, Guy 7:543
Johnston, Henrietta 7:543
joiners 2:136, 3:225–26
**Jolliet, Louis 4:281, 4:283,
5:340, 5:378, 5:391**
Jones, John Paul 2:122, 5:341
Jones, Philip 1:46
Josselyn, John 3:174
journeymen 1:33, 5:385, 9:702
Junto 1:54, 3:207, 9:672

K
Kean, Thomas 8:576
Keith, William 3:207
**Kentucky 3:186, 4:301,
5:342–43, 5:358**
Kidd, William 8:570
**King George's War 5:339,
5:344–45, 7:488–89, 7:549**
  Battle of Louisbourg
   5:344–45, 5:375–76
King Philip see Metacom
**King Philip's War 2:121,
5:346–49, 6:415, 6:438,
8:589, 9:645**
**King William's War
5:350–51, 7:487**
kiva 8:601
Knox, John 4:298
Kodiak Island 1:9, 8:630
Kosciuszko, Tadeusz 5:352
Kühn, Justus 7:540

L

La Mothe Cadillac, Antoine de **1**:50, **2**:*151*

La Salle, René-Robert Cavelier, Sieur de 3:212, **4**:283, **5**:*353*, **5**:*377*, **5**:378

Labrador **7**:520

lacrosse **2**:*98*, **3**:188, **3**:*230*

Lafayette, Marquis de 1:26, **1**:27, **5**:*354*

Lalemant, Charles **6**:448-50

Lamb, John **9**:*703*

land 4:279–80, **5**:*355–60*, **9**:*700–701*, **10**:*732*
   see also environment;
      farming; frontier

Lane, Ralph **9**:655

language and speech 1:13, **4**:280, **4**:297, **5**:*361–64*
   slave **9**:683–84, **9**:686

Las Casas, Bartolome de **9**:*693*

Laurens, Henry **2**:94, **7**:*544*

Laval, Francois de
      Montmorency **9**:668

Laval University **9**:668

Law, John **5**:378–79, **7**:504-05

Lawrence, Charles **1**:5

lawyers **2**:140, **9**:701

Le Caron, Joseph **6**:447

Le Moyne, Pierre **7**:488

Leather Apron Club *see* Junto

leather manufacture **5**:389

Lechmere, Thomas **4**:293

Lederer, John **5**:342

Lee, Arthur **3**:209

Lee, Charles **2**:94, **6**:*456*

Lee, Richard **9**:*702*

Lee, Richard Henry **2**:145–46

leeches **6**:423–24

Leisler's Rebellion 5:*365*, **7**:513, **7**:*517*

Lely, Peter **4**:*252*

letters of marque **8**:569, **8**:571

Lexington and Concord, Battles of 1:18, **2**:124, **2**:129, **5**:*366–67*, **6**:445

Liberty Bell 5:*368*

Liberty Boys *see* Sons of Liberty

libraries and books 1:*52–55*, **1**:71, **4**:*263*, **6**:422, **7**:521
   almanacs **1**:*53*, **1**:55, **6**:422, **6**:425, **7**:523–24
   see also Bible; newspapers;
      printing

Library of Congress **1**:53

Lincoln, Benjamin **9**:*664*, **9**:681

linen **4**:*310*

literacy **9**:666

livestock 3:184, **3**:186, **5**:*369–72*
   see also farming

Livingston, Robert **2**:*146*, **9**:700

Lloyd, David **8**:565

Locke, John 5:*373*, **9**:705

log cabins **1**:*34*, **1**:35, **2**:*150*, **3**:*205*, **7**:*509*

"Log College" **4**:300

Logan, James **1**:53, **8**:565

Long Island, Battle of 1:21, **4**:266, **5**:*374*

Lopez, Aaron **8**:619

Lost Colony *see* Roanoke

Loudon, Lord **3**:214

Louis XIV **4**:254, **7**:486, **8**:607
   and the colonization of New
      France **4**:*281*, **4**:283, **4**:*303*, **4**:305, **5**:*378*

Louisbourg 5:*375–76*, **7**:533, **7**:*535*
   Battle of (1745) **5**:344–45, **5**:*375–76*
   Battle of (1758) **3**:214, **5**:376, **7**:535

Louisiana 1:50, **3**:*165*, **3**:202, **5**:*377–80*
   cajuns **1**:5
   and La Salle **5**:*353*, **5**:377-8
   river travel **9**:650
   settlement **4**:284, **4**:306, **5**:360
   wheat **6**:444
   see also New Orleans

Louisiana Purchase **5**:338

Lowell, Francis Robert **6**:418

Loyalists 1:27–28, **3**:211, **4**:297, **5**:*381–83*

Lutherans **4**:*287*, **8**:616, **8**:617

M

McCawley, Elizabeth **4**:293

McDougall, Alexander **9**:703

Madison, James 2:109, **5**:*384*, **9**:*667–68*

Magellan, Ferdinand **7**:532

Makemie, Francis **8**:625

malaria **3**:165

Malinche **6**:*435*

Mance, Jeanne **6**:459

manufacturing 5:*385–90*, **6**:418

Maple Ceremony **3**:188

Mardi Gras **3**:191

markets **5**:369, **5**:372, **8**:566

maroons **3**:218

Marquette, Jacques 4:*281*, **4**:283, **5**:340, **5**:378, **5**:*391*

marriage 3:179, **3**:180, **6**:*404*-7, **8**:590
   indentured servants **4**:309
   intermarriages **3**:217–18, **6**:436–37, **8**:*591*, **8**:592, **9**:702
   Native Americans **6**:*404*, **8**:587–88
   slave **6**:407, **9**:685

Maryland 5:357, **6**:*408–12*
   border disputes **7**:547
   education **9**:666
   "exempt farms" **4**:291
   free blacks **3**:210
   government **4**:452, **6**:410-11
   indentured servants **4**:309
   Irish immigrants **4**:290–91
   merchants **6**:432
   milling **6**:442
   population growth **8**:591
   religion **2**:108–9, **6**:409–11, **8**:610, **8**:614–15
   slavery **9**:694, **9**:695–96
   see also Calvert, George;
      Chesapeake Bay area

Mason, George 6:*413*, **10**:760–61

Mason, John **7**:490

Massachuset **5**:346, **6**:414–15

Massachusetts 6:*414–18*
   coins **6**:417, **6**:453
   education in **9**:666
   food and drink **3**:198–99
   government **4**:250–51, **4**:252, **4**:255–56, **6**:417
   Government Act (1774) **5**:325
   Intolerable Acts **2**:128
   minutemen **6**:445
   no religious freedom **2**:107-8
   School Act (1647) **9**:666
   shipbuilding **3**:205
   slavery **9**:693–94
   State Constitution (1780) **1**:7
   voting in **9**:701
   see also Boston; Intolerable
      Acts; Massachusetts Bay
      Colony; Plymouth Colony
      and the Pilgrims

Massachusetts Bay Colony
      6:*414*, **6**:416
   faculty tax **10**:*732*
   first settlement **1**:58
   government **4**:279, **6**:416-17
   land allocation **5**:358
   livestock **5**:369
   marriage **6**:404, **6**:406, **6**:407
   migration of Puritans to **4**:277
   and Native Americans **5**:346
   and New Hampshire **7**:491
   Pequot War (1637) **5**:*346*, **6**:415
   settlers move to Connecticut **2**:119, **6**:416–17
   see also Puritans; Salem
      Witch Trials

Massachusetts Bay Company **6**:415, **6**:416

Massasoit, Chief **1**:14–15, **5**:*347*, **8**:580

Mather, Cotton 1:53, **1**:55, **3**:229, **6**:*419*, **6**:462, **8**:627
   and the Salem Witch Trials **6**:419, **9**:*657*, **9**:*658*

Mather, Increase **5**:349, **6**:419

May, Cornelius **7**:500

***Mayflower* 1**:65, **4**:276, **6**:*420–21*, **8**:578–79

Mayflower Compact **4**:279, **6**:*414*, **6**:*421*, **8**:579

Maynard, Robert **8**:571

medicine 2:95, **6**:*422–27*, **9**:*673–74*

medicine men *see* shamans

Membertou, Grand Chief **7**:534

Menendez, Francisco **9**:682–83

Mennonites **2**:*109*, **6**:404, **7**:548, **8**:616, **8**:*617*

mercantilism **5**:386–87, **6**:428–29, **10**:*742*, **10**:*747*

merchants 6:*428–33*, **8**:565–66, **8**:629, **9**:701, **9**:*702*, **9**:711, **10**:*746*
   see also manufacturing; trade

Mescalero **7**:499

mestizos **3**:217, **6**:435-6, **8**:592

Metacom 5:*347*, **5**:348–49, **6**:*434*, **9**:645
   see also King Philip's War

metalwork **2**:137–38

Methodism **4**:*258*, **4**:259

metis and mestizos 2:*133*, **3**:217, **3**:218, **6**:*435–37*, **8**:*591*, **8**:592

Middleton, Arthur **9**:*706*

midwives **6**:425

militia 2:*102*, **3**:189–90, **6**:*438–40*

milling 6:*441–44*

Minnesota **7**:531, **9**:*649*

Minuit, Peter **7**:501, **7**:509-11

minutemen 6:*445*

missionaries 6:*446–51*, **8**:614, **8**:621
   French **4**:281–82, **7**:485, **8**:614
   Spanish **2**:86–87, **4**:303–4, **7**:507, **8**:614, **8**:*615*, **9**:*693*
   see also Catholics; churches
      and missions

missions *see* churches and
   missions

Mississippi River **2**:*144*, **6**:444, **9**:*651*
   explored by de Soto **5**:377
   explored by Jolliet and
      Marquette **4**:*281*, **4**:283, **5**:340, **5**:378, **5**:391
   explored by La Salle **4**:283, **5**:*353*, **5**:*377*, **5**:378

Mittelberger, Gottlieb **4**:289

Mohegan **5**:346

Molasses Act (1733) **5**:388, **9**:*698*, **10**:728

money 6:417, **6**:*452–55*, **7**:494
   and bartering **6**:443, **6**:452–53
   commodity **6**:453-4, **10**:*732*
   forgers **2**:*140*

Monmouth, Battle of 1:*20*, **1**:24, **6**:*456*

Montcalm, Marquis de 3:214, **3**:215, **6**:*457*, **8**:603

Montgomery, Richard **1**:19–20

Monticello **5**:*338*

Montreal 2:88, **2**:91, **3**:215, **6**:*458*–61
   Battle of **3**:215, **6**:460–61

Moore, James **8**:607

Moore's Creek, Battle of **7**:*529*

Moravians **5**:389, **6**:451, **7**:548, **8**:*616*, **8**:*617*

Morgan, Daniel **9**:*708*

Morris, Lewis **7**:494–95

Moscoso, Luis de **2**:144

Moultrie, William **2**:94

Muhlenberg, Henry **8**:616

mulattos **6**:435, **6**:*436*

Murray, William **8**:576

Muscovy Company **4**:267

music 6:*462–65*, **9**:686

N

Narragansett **5**:346, **5**:348, **9**:*644*

Native Americans
   bathing **6**:*426*
   canoes **9**:650
   child-rearing **2**:105
   clothing **1**:*12*, **5**:*330*, **5**:331
   and the colonial militia **6**:*439*

and diseases **3**:164-66, **3**:171, **4**:273, **7**:507, **8**:588–89
distribution **1**:*11*, **1**:*30*, **2**:96, **5**:*329*
dreams and visions **8**:*623*
and European culture **5**:*333*
family life **3**:181, **8**:588-9
farming **3**:182–83, **3**:185, **3**:198, **4**:272, **5**:329–30, **5**:*355*, **6**:466–67
festivals **3**:188–89
fishing **3**:*170*, **3**:*193*
food preparation **3**:*198*, **3**:202
French and Indian War **3**:*212–15*
funeral rites **3**:221
fur trappers **3**:*223*, **3**:224
games **2**:*98*, **3**:188, **3**:*230*
homes **1**:30–31
and horses **5**:*371*, **10**:735
hunting by **4**:270, **8**:621
lands given to **3**:219
lands given up **2**:99, **5**:*343*, **7**:531
marriage **6**:*404*, **8**:587–88
medicine **3**:*166*, **6**:425, **6**:426
paintings **6**:467
population 8:*587–89*
pottery **2**:135
religion **1**:31, **3**:170, **4**:*272*, **8**:*620–23*, **10**:*730*
and rice **9**:648
shamans **1**:13, **3**:*166*, **8**:*622*, **8**:623
as slaves **8**:589, **9**:*692*, **9**:*693*
society **1**:13, **1**:31, **4**:*272*–73, **5**:*331*–33, **6**:*467*–68
and the Spanish **7**:507
supernatural beliefs **4**:*272*, **8**:621, **8**:622, **10**:*730*
trading **1**:15–16, **2**:*133*, **3**:*223*, **4**:273, **4**:282, **6**:*431*, **8**:587, **10**:*744*
villages **8**:*587*, **9**:676
visits to England **2**:*95*-97
wampum **6**:*453*
wigwams **1**:*12*, **1**:*13*, **9**:676, **9**:*678*
women **3**:181, **3**:*182*, **4**:273, **5**:331, **8**:588, **10**:*786*
words and language **1**:13, **5**:*363*
Navajo 6:*466–68*, **7**:*499*
naval stores 3:204–5, **6**:*469*
Navigation Acts 3:167, **5**:387, **6**:429–30, **6**:432, **6**:*470–71*, **10**:732–33, **10**:*744*, **10**:746
Neale, Thomas **8**:594
needlework **2**:134–35, **2**:*138*
New Albion **3**:168
New Amsterdam **4**:307, **7**:*501*, **7**:*503*, **7**:*511*, **7**:516, **10**:725
see also New York City
New Connecticut **10**:756
New England **4**:*279*
colonies *see* Connecticut; Massachusetts Bay Colony; Plymouth Colony and the Pilgrims; Rhode Island Confederation **8**:580

visited by Norsemen **6**:414
see also English immigration
New France 7:*484–89*
claimed by Cartier **2**:88, **2**:*89*
colonization **4**:281–82, **7**:*484*–85
defense policy **6**:438
education **9**:668
fur traders **2**:*132–33*, **3**:218, **3**:223, **4**:283, **10**:*743*
government **2**:114, **4**:254, **4**:257, **4**:283
and the Huron **2**:90, **2**:91, **4**:273, **4**:282, **7**:485
imperial policy **4**:*303*, **4**:304–6, **7**:*486*
Iroquois defeated **7**:486–88
mixed-race families **6**:436–37
population **4**:284, **7**:487, **8**:591–92
Protestants excluded **4**:284, **6**:*447*
settlement patterns **5**:360
social structure **9**:702
New Hampshire 1:17, **4**:*256*, **4**:299, **7**:*490–91*, **7**:491, **10**:732
New Jersey 7:*492–95*, **7**:513, **8**:*624*, **9**:669, **9**:*670*, **9**:694
government **4**:252, **7**:493–94
Scots-Irish immigrants **4**:299–300
New Mexico 7:*496–99*
Acoma **7**:*497*, **7**:498, **8**:601
buildings **1**:34–35, **7**:*496*, **7**:*498*
Native Americans **6**:468, **7**:498–99, **8**:589, **8**:597, **9**:661
New Netherland 4:307, **7**:*500–503*, **7**:510–11, **7**:516
architecture **1**:*37*
banks **6**:455
commodity money **6**:453
divided in two **7**:513
festivals **3**:191
government **7**:502–3
Jewish immigrants **8**:618
and language **5**:364
religions **7**:502, **8**:*613*, **8**:618
takeover by the English **7**:503, **7**:516
see also New Amsterdam; New York; New York City; Stuyvesant, Peter
New Orleans 1:50, **3**:*172*, **4**:283, **5**:379, **7**:*504–5*
New Spain 6:435–36, **7**:*506–8*
buildings **1**:34–36, **2**:86
clothing **2**:111
defense policy **6**:438
farming **3**:185–86
Georgia **4**:245
government **4**:254, **4**:257, **7**:506
imperial policy **4**:302–4, **7**:506–7
intermarriages **3**:217, **6**:436, **8**:*591*, **8**:592, **9**:702
Jewish immigrants **8**:618
and land **5**:*357*, **5**:358–59

Louisiana part of **5**:379–80, **7**:505
missionaries **2**:86, **4**:303–4, **6**:*446–47*, **7**:507, **8**:614, **8**:*615*
Native Americans **1**:31, **2**:99, **8**:*597–601*, **8**:*615*, **9**:*692*
Pacific coast explored **1**:*51*
Royal Highway **9**:654
slavery and the slave trade **9**:682–83, **9**:690, **9**:*692*
see also California; conquistadores; Florida; New Mexico; Texas
New Sweden 2:149, **2**:*149*, **4**:*307*, **7**:*509*, **10**:725
New Sweden Company **7**:509
New York 7:*510–15*
Anglicanism **2**:107
free blacks **3**:211
government **4**:252
immigrants **4**:289, **4**:297
slavery **9**:694
New York City 4:252, **7**:*513*, **7**:*516–19*, **8**:575
Jewish immigrants **8**:618
the Revolutionary War **1**:20–21, **4**:266, **5**:*374*, **7**:519
see also New Amsterdam
Newark, New Jersey **7**:493
Newfoundland 3:175, **3**:192, **7**:*520*
Newport, Christopher **5**:*334*
newspapers 7:*521–24*, **10**:*732*
Nicholson, Francis **2**:96, **5**:365
Nicot, Jean **10**:738
Niza, Marcos de **7**:496, **7**:497
Nonimportation Agreement **9**:711
North, Lord 7:*525*
North Carolina 4:297, **7**:*526–29*
Anglicanism **2**:107
education in **9**:666
Loyalists **5**:382
merchants **6**:432
naval stores **6**:469
plantations **8**:*572*, **9**:*649*
northeast passage, and Henry Hudson **4**:267
North-West Company **4**:269, **6**:437
Northwest Ordinance 7:*530–31*
Northwest Passage 4:267, **4**:281, **7**:500, **7**:*532*
Nova Scotia 5:383, **7**:487, **7**:488–89, **7**:*533–35*
see also Acadia; Cape Breton Island; Louisbourg

O

Oglethorpe, James 4:*245*, **4**:*247*, **4**:*258*, **4**:*297*, **7**:*536*
campaign against St. Augustine **2**:97, **3**:*197*, **9**:656
Ohio (state) **7**:531
Ohio Company **3**:212, **9**:679
Ohio Valley **1**:16, **3**:212, **3**:213, **5**:325, **8**:583, **9**:676–79

Ojibwa/Ojibway **1**:*11*, **1**:*13*, **9**:648
Old Northwest **7**:*530–31*
Oñate, Juan de 7:498, **7**:*537*, **8**:*600*–601
Oneida **1**:67
Opechancanough **8**:595
Osburn, Sarah **9**:658
Otermin, Antonio de **9**:662
Otis, James **6**:*418*
Ottawa (Native Americans) **1**:16, **3**:*214*
Outacity **2**:97

P

Paine, Thomas 5:367, **7**:*538–39*, **8**:594
painting 7:540–44, **9**:650
see also crafts
Pamlico tribe **7**:*528*
Paoli, Battle of **7**:*551*
Paris, Treaty of (1763) 1:5, **1**:6, **3**:215, **5**:379, **10**:*748*
and Florida **3**:197, **4**:247
and Louisiana **7**:505
and New France **7**:489
Paris, Treaty of (1783) 2:99, **2**:151, **3**:209, **7**:*544*, **9**:680, **10**:*749*
and Florida **3**:197, **5**:380
Parker, John **5**:*366*
Parker, Peter **2**:94
Parris, Samuel **9**:658, **9**:659
Pascal, Michael **3**:176
Paterson, William **2**:122
Patriots **2**:*143*, **6**:440
patroonships **7**:502
Paxton, Charles **1**:60
Paxton Boys **3**:219, **7**:550
Penn, William 2:109, **2**:149, **4**:*251*, **4**:287–88, **7**:*545*, **7**:549
and the growth of Philadelphia **8**:564, **8**:568
receives Pennsylvania charter **5**:*356*, **5**:357, **7**:546, **7**:547
Pennsylvania 4:*251*, **7**:*546–51*, **8**:590–91, **8**:*629*
English migrants in the minority **4**:280
granted to Penn **5**:*356*, **5**:357, **7**:546, **7**:547
immigrants **4**:285–88, **4**:*298*, **4**:300, **7**:548, **8**:619
Paxton Boys **3**:219, **7**:550
Quakers **8**:628–29
religious communities **4**:288, **7**:548, **8**:615, **8**:616–17, **8**:617, **8**:628–29
religious freedom **2**:*109*
University of/Philadelphia Academy **3**:208, **8**:551, **9**:670, **9**:672
see also Philadelphia
Pennsylvania Gazette **3**:207, **7**:523, **7**:*538*, **10**:*746*
Pepperell, William **5**:*345*, **5**:*375*
Pequot **1**:*15*, **2**:*121*, **5**:346
Pequot War (1637) **5**:*346*, **6**:415

Peralta, Pedro de **7**:498, **8**:601, **9**:661, **9**:662
Percival, John **4**:245
Percy, George **5**:335
Perez, Juan **1**:9
Peter, John Frederick **6**:464
Philadelphia 7:546, **7**:551, **8**:*564–68*
  Academy/Pennsylvania University **3**:208, **7**:551, **9**:670, **9**:672
  architecture **1**:39, **8**:*567*, **8**:568
  education **7**:551
  immigrants **4**:289, **4**:299–300
  Independence Hall **1**:39, **2**:145, **8**:567–68
  merchants **8**:565–66, **8**:629
  Philadelphia Library **3**:208
  theater **8**:*575*, **8**:576
Phips, William **3**:*216*, **5**:*350*, **5**:*351*, **9**:658
Pilgrims *see* Plymouth Colony and the Pilgrims
Pinckney, Eliza Lucas **5**:324, **8**:572
Pinenda, Alonso de **5**:377
pinnaces **9**:651
piracy 4:306, **7**:528, **8**:*569–71*, **10**:773–74
pirogues **9**:650
Piscataway **6**:408
Pitcairn, Major **5**:366–67
pitch **3**:204, **3**:206
Pitcher, Molly **6**:*456*
Pitt, William **3**:214, **3**:215
Pizarro, Francisco **4**:303
Plains of Abraham, Battle of **6**:457, **10**:*783*
Plantation Duty Act (1673) **6**:471
plantations 1:*71*, **5**:357, **8**:*572–73*, **9**:*701*
  crafts and workshops **5**:386, **5**:*387*
  education on **9**:666
  owners **1**:38-9, **1**:52–53, **1**:71, **2**:111, **8**:*572*, **9**:*700*, **9**:*706*
  slave freedom **3**:210
  slaves **8**:585, **8**:586, **9**:648–49, **9**:684–85, **9**:695–96
  see also cotton; indigo; rice; sugar; tobacco
plants, medicinal **6**:*425*, **6**:426
plays and theaters 8:*574–77*
plows **3**:186–87
Plymouth Colony and the Pilgrims 2:*106*, **4**:276, **6**:415–16, **8**:578, **8**:*578–80*
  children **2**:100
  clothing **2**:110
  farming **3**:183, **10**:736
  founders **6**:420–21
  governors *see* Bradford, William; Carver, John
  journey to America **1**:*65*, **4**:276, **4**:*305*, **6**:*414*, **6**:*420*–21
  livestock **5**:369
  Mayflower Compact **4**:279,

6:*414*, **6**:*421*, **8**:579
  meetinghouses **8**:*579*, **8**:*627*
  Native Americans **1**:14–15, **1**:*15*, **1**:65, **5**:*347*, **5**:348, **5**:*361*, **8**:580
  religious laws **2**:141
  see also Mayflower
Pocahontas 1:14, **5**:335, **8**:*581*, **9**:697
Ponce de León, Juan 3:196, **7**:*506*, **8**:*582*
Pontiac, Chief **1**:*16*, **3**:*214*, **8**:*583*
Pontiac's Rebellion **5**:339, **8**:*583*, **8**:*596*, **9**:679
Popé **8**:602
"Pope's Day" **3**:190
Popham Colony **3**:190
population **3**:218
  black *see* black population
  British **4**:276, **4**:280, **8**:590–91
  French **4**:284, **7**:487, **8**:591–92
  Native American 8:*587–89*
  Scots-Irish **4**:299
  Scottish **4**:297
  Spanish **8**:591–92
  white 8:*590–92*
Port Royal/Annapolis Royal **4**:281, **4**:*282*, **7**:484–85
postal service 8:*593–94*
potato famine, Irish **4**:293
Potomac Canal **9**:652
pottery **2**:*135*, **8**:*601*
Powhatan 8:*581*, **8**:*595*, **9**:697
Presbyterians 4:259, **8**:*624–25*
  and education **4**:300, **9**:668
  in Ulster **4**:299
  presbyteries **8**:624
Prescott, Samuel **8**:631
Prescott, William **1**:68
Preston, Thomas **1**:*62*
Pride, John **2**:135
Princeton College **4**:300, **7**:*494*, **9**:*670*
printing **1**:*32*, **1**:55, **7**:521
Printz, Johan **7**:509
privateers *see* piracy
Proclamation Line **8**:596
Proclamation of 1763 8:*596*
Protestant Episcopal Church **8**:611
Prouville, Alexandre de **7**:486
Prynne, Hester **2**:*143*
Pueblo 8:*597–601*
Pueblo Revolt 7:499, **8**:601, **8**:*602*, **9**:662
pueblos **1**:*35*, **7**:*498*, **8**:*597*, **8**:*598*, **8**:*599*
Puritans 4:277, **8**:*626–27*, **10**:729–30
  and Boston citizens **1**:58-9
  buildings **1**:36
  and celebrations **3**:189, **3**:*191*, **3**:*230*
  children **2**:102-3
  church-government relations **2**:106–8
  clothing **2**:110
  family life **3**:179–80
  funerals **3**:220

  the Great Awakening **8**:627
  marriage **6**:405, **6**:*406*, **6**:407
  and missionary work **6**:450-1
  Moderates and Theocrats **1**:59
  and music **6**:462
  and paintings **7**:540
  and sports **3**:229, **3**:*230*
  and taxation **9**:699
  Thanksgiving **3**:190–91, **8**:580, **10**:736–37
  and theater-going **8**:574
  see also Massachusetts Bay Colony; Mather, Cotton; Plymouth Colony and the Pilgrims; Salem Witch Trials
Purman, Lucy **6**:407

Q

Quakers 8:*628–29*, **9**:699, **10**:*788*
  and books **1**:53
  child-rearing **2**:100
  clothing **2**:*112*
  marriage **6**:404, **6**:405
  in Maryland **6**:410
  meeting houses **6**:*410*, **7**:*493*, **7**:*516*
  New Jersey **7**:492–93, **7**:494
  in Pennsylvania **7**:548–50
  and Puritan intolerance **2**:107
  in Rhode Island **9**:645
  and slavery **8**:629, **9**:696
  see also Penn, William
Quartering Act **5**:325
Quebec (province) **3**:229–30, **4**:281, **4**:284, **9**:668
Quebec, Battle of (1759) 3:215, **6**:457, **8**:*603*
Quebec, Battle of (1775) **1**:*20*, **6**:461
Quebec Act (1774) **5**:325, **5**:382
Quebec City 2:*91*, **2**:*114*, **7**:*485*, **8**:*604–6*
  education in **9**:668
  and King William's War **5**:*351*
  missionaries **6**:448–49
  siege of (1690) **3**:216
Queen Anne's War 2:148, **7**:488, **8**:*607–8*
quilts **2**:*138-9*
quitrent system **5**:355
Quivira **2**:131

R

race, mixed *see* metis and mestizos
Radisson, Pierre **4**:268
Raleigh, Walter 3:168, **8**:*609*, **9**:*655*, **10**:*738*
Rall, Johann **10**:751
ranches **5**:359
Randolph, Edmund **2**:122
Rasles, Sebastian **1**:15
Read, George **2**:150
Recollects **6**:447–48, **7**:485
redemptioners **4**:288
Reformed Church **8**:616, **8**:617
Regulators **7**:528–29, **9**:681, **9**:707

religion
  church-state relations 2:*106*–9, **4**:278
  religious revival *see* Great Awakening
  religious toleration **2**:108, **2**:109, **4**:248, **6**:409–10
  and women **10**:787–88
  see also churches and missions; supernatural; and under various religions
Remington, Frederick **6**:448
Rensselaer, Kiliaen Van **7**:502, **9**:700
resin **3**:204, **3**:206, **6**:469
Revere, Paul 1:18, **1**:*33*, **1**:*61*, **5**:366, **8**:*631*
  pictures by **1**:*62*, **5**:*325*
  and the Sons of Liberty **9**:703
Revolutionary War *see* American Revolutionary War
Rhode Island 9:*644–47*, **10**:*765*, **10**:*780*
  founded **8**:*612*, **9**:644–45
  government **4**:249, **4**:253
  Jewish immigrants **8**:618-9
  merger with Connecticut **2**:120
  and Nathanael Greene **4**:*260*
  Newport **1**:39, **8**:*618*, **8**:619, **9**:645, **9**:*646*
  Providence **8**:*612*, **9**:644-6
  Quakers **8**:628
  religious toleration **2**:108, **4**:274, **9**:645
  settlers from Massachusetts **6**:417, **9**:645
  trade **6**:471
rice 4:247, **8**:572, **9**:*648–49*, **9**:706–7, **10**:744
Richelieu, Cardinal **7**:485-6
Rijswijk, Treaty of **5**:351
Rind, William **1**:55
Rio Grande **7**:*498*, **7**:*537*
Rising, Johan **7**:509
Rittenhouse, David **8**:566, **9**:*673*
river travel 9:*650–52*
roads 5:372, **6**:443, **8**:593, **8**:594, **9**:*653–54*
Roanoke settlement 4:*277*, **7**:526–27, **8**:609, **9**:*655*, **10**:757
Roberval, Sieur de **2**:89
Rochambeau, Comte de **1**:26-7
Roebuck, Colonel **1**:23
Roger's Raiders **3**:*215*
Rolfe, John **5**:335, **8**:*581*, **10**:739, **10**:758
Royall, Isaac **9**:690
Rush, Benjamin **6**:427, **9**:674
Russian Orthodoxy 8:*630*
Rutledge, John **2**:94

S

Sagard, Gabriel **2**:105
Saguenay **2**:88, **2**:89
St. Augustine 3:*197*, **7**:*507*, **7**:536, **9**:*656*, **10**:724
  and Queen Anne's War **8**:607-08
St. Clair, Arthur **7**:*494*

St. Lawrence, Gulf of **2**:89, **2**:90
St. Nicholas's Day **3**:189, **3**:191
St. Patrick's Day **3**:190
Salem Witch Trials **6**:417, **6**:419, **9**:657–60
Samoset **5**:361
San Antonio, Texas **10**:735
Santa Fe **7**:496, **7**:498, **9**:661–62
Saratoga, Battle of **1**:23, **1**:70, **2**:127, **5**:352, **7**:515, **9**:663–64
Sassamon, John **5**:348
Sauer, Christopher **8**:617
schools and colleges **2**:103, **9**:665–70
  Anglican **8**:610–11
  Baptist **8**:613
  libraries **1**:53
  'Log Colleges' **4**:300
  medical schools **6**:427
  in New Spain **7**:507–8
  in Pennsylvania **7**:551
  Presbyterian **4**:300, **8**:625
  Scots-Irish **4**:300
Schuyler, Philip John **1**:17, **9**:663, **9**:664
Schwenkfelders **7**:548, **8**:617
science **6**:427, **9**:671–74
Scots-Irish immigration **3**:203, **4**:298–301, **8**:625
Scott, Peter **3**:227
Scottish immigration **4**:294–97
Second Dutch War **2**:149
Sedition Act (1798) **1**:6
seigneurs **6**:460, **9**:702
selectmen **4**:255–56
serfs **9**:687–88
Serra, Junipero **9**:675
servants **2**:112, **3**:210, **9**:695
  see also free blacks; indentured servants
Seven Years' War **3**:212, **10**:748
"shallops" **9**:650
shamans (medicine men) **1**:13, **3**:166, **8**:622, **8**:623
Sharp, Granville **9**:696
Shawnee **1**:56, **5**:342, **9**:676–79
Shays's Rebellion **9**:680–81
sheep **5**:370–71
Shelikhov, Gregorii **1**:9
shellfish **3**:194, **3**:200, **3**:202
sheriffs **4**:256
Sherman, Robert **7**:544
Sherman, Roger **2**:146
ships **6**:432, **6**:471, **9**:651
shipbuilding **3**:205, **5**:390, **6**:418, **6**:469
Shirley, Governor **5**:344
Shirley plantation **1**:38, **3**:200
Shuckburg, Dr. Richard **6**:465
Simons, Menno **8**:616
Sioux, Sun Dance **8**:620
slave culture **3**:181, **9**:682–86, **10**:730
  burials **3**:221
  kinship **3**:181, **9**:684–85
  language **5**:364, **9**:684–85, **9**:694

marriage **6**:407
music/dancing **6**:465, **8**:586, **9**:686
slave trade **2**:123, **3**:177, **8**:584–85, **9**:687–90, **9**:691, **10**:745
  and piracy **8**:570
  and Rhode Island **9**:646
  ships **3**:177, **9**:688, **9**:689–90
  the Triangular Trade **5**:388, **9**:689–90
slavery **3**:210, **9**:691–96, **10**:724
  antislavery campaign **5**:368, **9**:696
  and Caribbean plantations **8**:585, **8**:586, **9**:693–96
  children **2**:100, **8**:585, **9**:669
  clothing **2**:112
  diseases of **3**:165, **3**:166
  and education **9**:669
  ending **9**:690, **9**:696, **10**:756, **10**:761
  escaping **2**:143, **3**:197, **3**:218
  freedom from **2**:150, **3**:210, **9**:686
  indentured servants replaced by **4**:311, **5**:693
  laws of **9**:693–94
  of Native Americans **8**:589, **9**:692, **9**:693
  Quaker beliefs **8**:629
  sick slaves **6**:426–27
  slaves' Loyalist sympathies **5**:382–83
  and taxation **2**:123, **10**:732
  and the timber industry **3**:205
  uneven distribution **8**:585
  women **10**:787
  see also black population; plantations; slave culture; slave trade; Stono Rebellion
Sloughter, Henry **5**:365
smallpox **3**:164–65, **3**:171, **6**:419
Smith, Francis **5**:366, **5**:367
Smith, James **4**:300
Smith, John **1**:58, **4**:279, **5**:334, **8**:581, **9**:697, **10**:758
  and fishing **3**:231
  and Massachusetts **6**:414–15
smuggling **6**:433, **7**:508, **9**:698–99, **10**:774
social structure **9**:700–702, **9**:708
Societe Notre Dame **6**:458–59
Society for the Propagation of the Gospel **8**:610
soldiers
  uniforms **1**:26, **6**:440
  see also Continental Army; Hessians; militia
Sons of Liberty **2**:117, **7**:515, **9**:703–4, **9**:710
South Carolina **9**:705–8
  Anglicanism **2**:107
  colonial assembly **4**:251
  education in **9**:666
  free blacks **3**:210
  immigrants **4**:300, **8**:619, **9**:706

local government **4**:256
Loyalists **5**:382
merchants **6**:432
plantations **8**:572, **8**:573, **9**:695, **9**:706–7, **10**:772
slave uprising see Stono Rebellion
slavery **2**:143, **4**:311, **9**:685, **9**:686, **9**:690, **9**:706
  see also Charleston
southwest passage **7**:532
Spain **4**:254, **4**:302–4, **7**:506–7, **9**:699, **10**:742
  see also New Spain
Spanish Succession, War of **7**:488, **8**:607
sports see games and sports
Spotswood, Alexander **3**:199–200, **6**:439, **10**:781
Squanto **3**:183, **5**:361, **10**:736
Stadacona **8**:604
stagecoaches **9**:654
Stagg, Charles and Mary **8**:576
"Stalking Turkey" **2**:95
Stamp Act (1765) **7**:514–15, **9**:703, **9**:709–11, **10**:731, **10**:733
  and newspapers **7**:524, **10**:732
  and Patrick Henry **4**:265, **10**:731
  and the **Sons of Liberty** **2**:117, **7**:515, **9**:703–4, **9**:710
Stamp Act Congress **7**:515, **7**:519
Standish, Myles **6**:420–21
Stark, John **1**:22, **9**:664
Steuben, Augustus von **2**:127, **10**:754
Stiegel, Henry William **2**:138–39
Stoddard, Solomon **8**:627
Stone, William **6**:410
Stono Rebellion **9**:656, **10**:724
Stuart, James **4**:260
Stuart, John **9**:707
Stuyvesant, Peter **7**:502, **7**:503, **7**:511–12, **7**:516, **10**:725
  Baptists **8**:613
  Jewish immigration **8**:618
  Swedish colonists **7**:509, **10**:725
succotash **5**:330
sugar **10**:726–28
  plantations **4**:310, **8**:585, **8**:586, **9**:695, **10**:775–76
  smuggling molasses **9**:698-9
  trade in **6**:431, **9**:698, **9**:699, **10**:744–45
Sugar Act (1764) **1**:7, **1**:60–61, **6**:418, **6**:470, **9**:699
Sullivan, John **5**:333, **5**:374
supernatural **10**:729–30
  see also religion
surgery **6**:424–25
Susquehannock **1**:44
sweat baths **6**:426
Swedish settlers see New Sweden

switchel **2**:135
synagogues **8**:618, **8**:619
Syng, Philip, Jr. **9**:673

T
tailors **5**:386
Talon, Jean **7**:487
Tangier Island **5**:361–62, **5**:363
Tanos **9**:662
tar **3**:204, **3**:206
Tarleton, Colonel **9**:708
taverns and inns **3**:199, **3**:231
taxes **3**:215, **10**:731–33
  and commodity money **6**:453–54, **10**:732
  enumerated goods **6**:470–71, **9**:649, **9**:699
  on Massachusetts farmers **9**:680
  on molasses **9**:698, **10**:728
  on printed matter see Stamp Act (1765)
  quitrent system **5**:355
  and slavery **2**:123, **10**:732
  on tea **1**:61, **1**:63–64
  on tobacco **9**:698–99, **10**:731
  see also Townshend Taxes
tea **1**:61, **1**:63–64, **3**:201
  see also Boston Tea Party
Teach, Edward **7**:528, **8**:571
Tecumseh **7**:531
telescopes **9**:673
Tennessee, immigrants **4**:301
tepees see wigwams/tepees
Tewa **9**:662
Texas **10**:734–35
textiles **2**:134–35, **5**:389
Thanksgiving **3**:190–91, **3**:200, **3**:202, **8**:580, **10**:736–37
theaters see plays and theaters
Theocrats **1**:59
Thirty Years' War **4**:286
Thomson, Charles **4**:262, **4**:300
Three-Fifths Compromise **2**:123
Ticonderoga see Fort Ticonderoga
timber see wood
Tituba **9**:658
Tlingit **1**:8, **5**:327
tobacco **1**:44, **3**:185, **10**:738–40, **10**:744, **10**:775
  at Jamestown **5**:335, **10**:739
  as commodity money **6**:453–54, **10**:732
  merchants **6**:429, **6**:432
  and slaves **3**:210, **8**:572, **9**:695–96, **10**:739
  smuggling **9**:698–99
Toleration Act (1649) **2**:108, **2**:109, **6**:409–10
Toleration Act (1689) **4**:248
tombstones **3**:220, **3**:225
Tomochichi **4**:247
Tonty, Henri de **5**:331, **5**:353
Townshend Taxes **10**:741
Townshend Acts (1767) **1**:7, **1**:63, **6**:418, **10**:733
toys **2**:103, **3**:228–29
trade **1**:60, **10**:742–47
  bartering **6**:443, **6**:452–53

by river **9**:651–52
enumerated goods **6**:470–71,
9:649, **9**:699
and mercantilism **5**:386–87,
6:428–29, **10**:742, **10**:747
with Native Americans **1**:15,
1:16, **6**:428, **6**:431
and the Nonimportation
Agreement **9**:711
and **smuggling 9**:698–99
sugar **6**:431, **9**:698, **9**:699,
10:744–45
tobacco **9**:698–99, **10**:744
Triangular **5**:388, **9**:689–90
see also fur trade; merchants;
Navigation Acts; taxes
trappers see fur trade
travel see river travel; roads
trees see forestry
Trenton, Battle of 1:21–22,
4:261, **7**:495, **10**:**750–52**
Trumbull, John **4**:256
Tryon, William **7**:515, **7**:528–29
turkeys **3**:202, **4**:271
turpentine **3**:204, **3**:206, **6**:469
Tuscarora **1**:67, **5**:328–29
tutors **9**:666

U

Ulloa, Antonio de **7**:505
Ulster **4**:298–99, **4**:300
Union, Act of (1707) **4**:294–95
Urratia, Jose de **9**:662
Utrecht, Treaty of (1713) **1**:4,
4:269, **6**:459, **7**:488, **7**:520,
8:608

V

Vaca, Alvar Cabeza de **5**:377,
7:496, **10**:734
Valley Forge 1:24, **2**:127,
10:**753–54**, **10**:770
Vancouver, George **7**:532
Vargas, Diego de **7**:499, **8**:601,
8:602, **9**:662
Vassa, Gustavus **3**:176–77
Vaudreuil, Marquis de **6**:457
Vermont 1:17, **10**:**755–56**
Verrazano, Giovanni **4**:281,
4:304–5, **7**:492, **9**:644
Vikings **7**:533
Virginia 1:37, **1**:38, **10**:**757–62**
boats **9**:650, **9**:651–52
Burgesses see House of

Burgesses
commodity money **6**:454
courts **2**:141, **4**:256
currency **6**:454
declaration of rights **6**:413,
10:761
education in **9**:666
food and drink **3**:198–99
free blacks **3**:210, **3**:211
government **4**:249, **4**:251,
4:253, **4**:254, **4**:256
Governor De La Warr **2**:149,
4:253, **5**:334–35
hunting in **4**:270
immigration **10**:758–59
indentured servants **4**:311,
9:692
land purchased **5**:357
marriage in **6**:404
merchants **6**:432
mills **6**:441–42
Native Americans **8**:587,
9:650, **10**:757, **10**:759
plantations **1**:38–39, **1**:71,
5:357, **8**:573, **9**:700
Popham Colony **3**:190
religion **2**:109, **8**:610, **8**:612
Scots-Irish immigrants **4**:301
slavery **9**:694, **9**:695–96,
10:758, **10**:759, **10**:761
tobacco **3**:185, **5**:357, **10**:731,
10:738–39, **10**:744
see also Chesapeake Bay
area; Jamestown; Roanoke
settlement; Williamsburg
Virginia Company 2:140,
4:253, **5**:334, **5**:335, **10**:738,
10:757–58, **10**:**763**
Virginia Conventions **4**:265,
5:384, **10**:760
Virginia Plan **2**:122, **5**:384
voting 9:701, **10**:**764–67**

W

Wadsworth, Joseph **2**:120
wagons **2**:137, **9**:654
Walker, John **9**:670
Walker, Zachariah **8**:625
Walum Olum **9**:676
Wampanoag **5**:346, **8**:580,
10:736–37
wampum **5**:328, **5**:329, **6**:453
Wamsutta **5**:347, **6**:434
Wappinger **7**:510

Washington, George 2:122,
3:228, **7**:524, **10**:762,
10:**768–70**
French and Indian War **3**:213,
10:768–69
and the Potomac Canal **9**:652
and the Proclamation Line
8:596
Revolutionary War **1**:18–24,
1:28, **2**:124–27, **6**:456,
7:495, **10**:750–54, **10**:769–70
servants **2**:112
watermills **6**:441, **6**:442, **6**:443
Wayne, Anthony **7**:530-1, **7**:551
weaving **2**:134, **6**:466-8
weddings **6**:405–6
see also marriage
Wesley, Charles **4**:258
Wesley, John **4**:258
West, Benjamin **7**:542–43,
7:544
**West Indies and the
Caribbean 2**:116, **4**:306–7,
10:**771–76**
indentured servants **4**:310
Irish immigration to **4**:290,
4:291, **4**:310–11
plantations **4**:291, **4**:310,
8:585, **8**:586, **10**:726–28,
10:772, **10**:774, **10**:775–76
slave trade **5**:388, **9**:688–89
slavery **8**:585, **8**:586,
9:693–96, **10**:726–28
sugar smuggling **9**:698
tobacco **10**:739, **10**:775
Westover Plantation **1**:38–39,
1:71, **9**:700
whaling 6:417, **9**:646,
10:**777–78**
wheat **3**:183–85, **6**:444
Wheatley, Phillis **10**:787
Wheelock, Eleazar **6**:451
White, Andrew **6**:450–51
White, John **1**:52, **7**:527, **9**:655
Whitefield, George 3:169,
4:258, **4**:259, **10**:**779**
wigwams/tepees **1**:12, **1**:13,
9:676, **9**:678
Wilderness Road **1**:57, **3**:218,
5:342–43
William III/William of Orange
1:59, **4**:248, **5**:350, **5**:365,
7:520
William and Mary, College of

9:669, **9**:670, **9**:671
Williams, Eunice **2**:148
Williams, John **2**:148
Williams, Roger 2:108, **4**:280,
8:612, **9**:644–45, **10**:**780**
Williamsburg 1:39, **2**:108,
10:760, **10**:**781**
windmills **6**:441–42, **6**:443
wine **3**:185, **3**:200
Winnebago **5**:377, **5**:379
Winslow, Edward **6**:420, **6**:421
Winthrop, John 1:58, **2**:107,
5:369, **6**:414, **6**:416, **6**:422,
10:**782**
Winthrop, John, Jr. **6**:418,
6:423, **7**:503
witchcraft **6**:425
see also Salem Witch Trials
witchdoctors see shamans
Witherspoon, John **4**:296,
9:670
Wolfe, James 3:215, **5**:376,
6:457, **8**:603, **10**:**783**
women's roles 3:178, **3**:181,
6:406, **6**:452, **10**:**784–88**
crafts **2**:134–35, **2**:136-9,
5:389, **5**:390, **10**:785
and farming **3**:186, **4**:308
girls' education **9**:666–67
indentured servants **4**:309,
10:784
Native American **3**:181,
3:182, **4**:273, **5**:331, **8**:588,
10:786
see also family life; marriage
wood **3**:204, **3**:205, **3**:227
see also forestry
woodwork **2**:136–37
wool **2**:136, **5**:370, **5**:390

Y

Yale University **2**:121
Yankee Doodle (song) **6**:465
Yazoo **5**:379
Yoacomaco **6**:408
Yorktown, Battle of 1:24,
1:26–27, **1**:28, **2**:130, **7**:524,
10:781, **10**:**789–90**

Z

Zenger, John Peter 7:523,
7:524, **10**:**791**
Zuni **7**:496, **7**:497, **8**:597,
8:600, **8**:601

**The editors wish to thank Peter Wallenstein, Associate
Professor of History at Virginia Polytechnic Institute and
State University, for his help in preparing this volume.**

Picture Credits
The American Museum in Britain, Bath 104b, 135, 136b, 138b
The Bridgeman Art Library 147 American Museum, Bath 134b
Christie's Images 111b David David Gallery, Philadelphia 128
Museum of Fine Art, Boston 117 National Gallery of Art,
Washington D.C.119 Earl of Radnor Collection, Wiltshire 110
Christie's Images 101 **Conneticut Historical Society,
Hartford** 142t **Corbis**/Bettmann 103t, 106, 118, 125t, 132b, 138-9t,
142b Library of Congress cover Jim Corwen 87t Historical Picture
Archive 136t David Muench 85t, 120b, 131b Gianni Dagli Orti 112t

Phil Schermeister 121b Lee Snider 93t, 108t, 149tr, 150 Tim
Thompson 96-7 Nik Wheeler 109 **ET Archive** 85b, 97 **Mary
Evans Picture Library** 86, 99, 100, 103b, 107bl, 108b, 114t, 116b,
120t, 123, 129b, 134t, 143 **Angelo Hornak Library** 102b, 129t
Hulton Getty 89t, 149tc **Peter Newark's American Pictures**
front cover, title page, 84, 88c, 88-9b, 90, 91, 92cl, 92-3b, 94, 95,
102t, 104t,107br, 111t, 113, 115, 116t, 122, 124, 125b, 126b, 127,
130, 131t, 133, 137, 140b, 141, 144, 145, 146, 148,151

Maps by John Woolford: 87, 96, 144
Artworks by John Egan: 98, 112, 132